Sold-Out Stewardship

How To Be Committed Caretakers of God's Blessings

Major A. Stewart

sermonto**book**
.com

Sermon To Book
www.sermontobook.com

Sold-Out Stewardship / Major A. Stewart
ISBN-13: 978-1-945793-03-5
ISBN-10: 1-945793-03-1

Praise for *Sold-Out Stewardship*

Dr. Stewart's book on *Sold-Out Stewardship* challenges every believer to shift their thinking and informs their faith back to a place of responsibility versus entitlement. ... When we embrace the kingdom mindset and put aside ego, we lose the country club mentality and are fully inducted into God's beloved community of stewardship!

—*Rev. Albert P. Jackson, M.Div.*
Senior Pastor, Ebenezer Baptist Church, Alexandria, Va.

Insightful, impactful, honest, revelatory, life-changing, and mind-blowing! ... This purposeful book is a must-have!

—*Deborah Payne-Stewart*
Executive Administrator, North Las Vegas, Nev.

Sold-Out Stewardship, provides the information, instruction, and inspiration to be better stewards so our lives bring greater glory to God. It's spiritual food for any Christian hungry to be a committed caretaker of His blessings!

—*Lorna Barrett*
TV news journalist and creator of News For Your Soul.com

In *Sold-Out Stewardship*, Dr. Stewart draws us in with his unique brand of humor to begin the careful and balanced handling of Kingdom finances and Christian stewardship. ... It is a masterful blend of biblical insight, Kingdom truths and refreshing wit!

—*Rev. Cheryl A. Carter, ND*
Associate Pastor, Mt. Sinai Baptist Church, Mansfield, Ohio

Sold-Out Stewardship breathes fresh understanding into an age-old biblical mandate, with well-chosen scriptural prescriptions, a relatable slice of life illustrations, and practical action steps for any Christian seeking spiritual maturity in the management of God's abundant blessings entrusted to our care.

—*Dr. Michael Andrew Owens*
Senior Pastor, Bethel Baptist Church, East Detroit, Mich.

Sold-Out Stewardship is a thought-provoking and eye-opening journey through the responsibilities, benefits, and blessings of biblical stewardship. Not only is this book a great personal benefit, it will also serve as a great teaching tool for any pastor/preacher who is trying to encourage stewardship among the believers!

—*Rev. Daniel Moore, Sr., M.Div.*
Pastor, Shiloh Missionary Baptist Church of Flint, Mich.

[This book] lays out for the believer, church member, church leaders and pastors, God's clear instruction on how we are to steward the resources God has given us. *Sold-Out Stewardship* is a great instruction manual for every Christian church.

—*Pastor David Washington, Jr.*
Founder & Lead Pastor, Canton Christian Fellowship Church, Canton, Mich.

Once again Dr. Major Stewart has displayed his acute exegesis and precise articulation. The readers of this treatise will inevitably receive profound information and spiritual inspiration!

—*Pastor Alfred L. Harris, Sr.*
Saints of God Church, Flint, Mich.

First and foremost, I would like to thank God. In the process of putting this book together, I realized how true this gift of writing is for me. You have given me the power to believe in my passion and pursue my dreams. I could never have done this without the faith I have in You, my Lord and Savior.

My family—my wife, Carla, and my daughters: – You are my #1 fans, and for that I am eternally grateful.

My parents—Annie Mae Stewart, Ruby Dale Fletcher, Jessie D. York & Albert Stewart – Because of you, I am!

My grandparents—Pearl Skipwith and Chester Vaughn; Sylvia and William York – Thank you for good genes.

Mr. John Barrett—I learned the stewardship of home life by observing how you cared for your family, home, and yard.

Mr. Don Cole – I learned the stewardship of mentoring the less fortunate by observing how you mentored me and others.

Coach Glen Metcalf – I learned the stewardship of teamwork under your leadership.

My nephew Frederick "Ricky" Stewart and my cousin Roy Gray – You both taught me the stewardship of family. You were always there for me—no matter what.

Ms. Sadie Mae Williams – You have always been a pillar of strength in our family.

Ms. Dorothy McDaniel – Because of your passion for typing, I was encouraged to push on. In part, this book is the result of learning the skill of typing.

Mr. Malcolm Stevens – I learned the stewardship of leadership and productivity under your leadership.

Mr. Mark Glover – I learned the stewardship of practical knowledge as you taught me how to apply chemistry to life.

Ms. Gerri Hall – You were my very first professional mentor. You taught me the stewardship of corporate and personal branding.

Mr. Johnny Bankhead – I learned the stewardship of education from you. I will always be indebted to you for inviting me to go to school with you in the first grade, while I was sitting on a Spring Street curb in Muskegon, Michigan.

Mrs. Linda Gill-MacFarland – I learned the stewardship of friendship and loyalty from you.

Mr. Robert Dowson – I learned the stewardship of family roots and the importance of family reunions from you.

Coach Ray Murdaugh – I learned the stewardship of discipline as I observed how you managed the Port City Rockets from the sideline.

Dr. Jim Hinga – I learned the stewardship of Christian education from you.

Steele Jr. High Fellas – I learned the stewardship of friendship from you all: Rafi Muhammad, Eddis Jones, Cedric "Rick" Jones, Johnny Bankhead, Bill Cowherd (deceased), Arthur Duren, Lou Knight, Kenny Childers, Joe "Al Capone" Johnson and Rodney Woods (deceased).

CONTENTS

Note from the Author

Thank you for purchasing *Sold-Out Stewardship*!

Accompanying each main chapter of the book is a set of reflective questions with an application-oriented summary provided as an "action step." These workbook sections are a tool to help you understand the biblical principles of stewardship and practice them in your management of the many blessings—financial and otherwise—with which God fills your life.

I recommend you go through these workbook sections with a pen in order to write your thoughts and record notes in the areas provided. The questions are suitable for independent reflection, discussion with a friend, or review with a study group.

Regardless of what led you to this book or how you choose to approach it, I hope that the experience of reading and reflecting about godly stewardship leads you to live fully for Christ, as He gave Himself fully to you.

—*Major A. Stewart*

INTRODUCTION

Spiritual Food

Many of us think the church only wants our money. But let's stop for a moment and think about this. When we go to the grocery store, do we say, "This store just wants my money"? When we go to buy a new car, do we say, "General Motors just wants my money?" When we go to the mall, do we say, "The mall just wants my money?" We don't say this about the grocer or the car dealer or the mall, because that's not the issue. The issue is that we need food and the grocery store has it. The value we place on the food we need makes it logical for us to pay for it. We need a car to get us where we need to go, so it makes sense to buy a vehicle. We need clothes, so we go to the mall to purchase some. In other words, it's not that these places just want our money; they are actually providing something we need.

What do we need from the church? Here are just some of the things: we need to be taught a word from the Lord; we need spiritual help; we need fellowship with other believers; we need training for our children; we need to know God's way; we need somebody to bury and marry our loved ones, and we need somebody to dedicate our babies.

If we go willingly to the grocery store for physical food, we ought to be willing to go to the house of God for spiritual food without whining about it.

So the question is not, "Does the church want our money?" Rather, the question is, "Does the church serve good food? Does it provide meaningful ministry opportunities? Are the sermons, the Bible studies and the Sunday school feeding us spiritually?" When we go to a good restaurant we don't mind paying for the food when it is good. And even when it's not so good, we still pay the bill and leave a tip.

We all need God. We need to hear from His Word. We need spiritual direction and enlightenment. We need fellowship from the body of Christ. We need biblical teaching for our children. We need somebody to marry and bury our loved ones. We need somebody to dedicate our babies. We even need somebody to birth us from time to time.

If we can go to the grocery store and buy physical food, we ought to be able to come to God's house for spiritual food—and offer Him something of ourselves in return.

Beyond tithing, however, we need to take an inventory of our spiritual condition, to re-examine what it means to be a church sold out to Jesus Christ or a believer on fire for the Lord. We need a stewardship self-assessment.

What is stewardship, and what does it have to do with our spiritual life? The Merriam-Webster dictionary tells us that stewardship is "the management of someone else's finances, property, or other affairs." So in spiritual terms, stewardship is the management of the finances, property, and other affairs that God has entrusted to us. All things belong to God, but He has appointed us to be the guardians or trustees over His estate. We have free reign with those resources, but will ultimately be held accountable to Him, by Him, according to the guidelines provided in the Bible (1 Corinthians 4:2).

There is no better way to evaluate our level of Christian maturity, our love for the Lord, and our desire to do His will than to look at the way we use those resources. If we want to see just how sold-out to God we are, we need to look at the way we use our time, our money, our relationships, our opportunities, our material possessions, our gifts, our abilities, and our energy.

Sold-out stewardship entails looking at the concept of biblical stewardship from a holistic perspective or mindset. According to George Barna, in his book *The Habits of Highly Effective Churches*, "holistic stewardship integrates biblical perspectives and principles on stewardship into all teaching and preaching."[1] In other words, genuine or true stewardship is not simply a lecture series or sermon series preached or taught during a specific time of the year. It is a part of the DNA and fabric of the church. It is a part of many sermons and many lessons throughout the course of the calendar year.

Holistic stewardship means that stewardship principles—both financial and non-monetary—are taught, included, or alluded to in sermons, lessons, and dramatic presentations throughout the course of the year. By incorporating stewardship concepts into sermons and lessons on other topics, the congregation is more frequently reminded about ways of interrelating key faith perspectives for thinking and living in a holistic and comprehensive Christian manner.[2]

Have we ever wondered why the church seems so powerless in the world? Let us consider that only eight percent of Christians even tithe. If we wonder why evil so dominates our culture and why Halloween is a bigger deal than Easter, we could note that only one out of four Christians actually attend church on any Sunday other than Easter. In other words, there is a direct correlation between our use of God's resources and our spiritual condition.

If we're going to be the church God has called us to be, we must be willing to give not just some of ourselves, not ten percent of ourselves, but all of ourselves to Christ.

CHAPTER ONE

It's Not Just about Money

Marketing experts tell us that "new and improved" will sell. We walk down an aisle in the supermarket and we find new and improved soap, new and improved detergent. We browse the shelves of Home Depot in search of a new and improved wrench. That's why some of us are driving new vehicles and wearing new shoes. Everybody knows something about "new and improved." And we serve a God who wants us to have a new and improved concept of what it means to be a good steward.

When Paul wrote to the church in Corinth, he told them it was required of stewards to be found faithful. A steward was someone who managed the property and affairs belonging to somebody else. As stewards in the body of Christ, we need to be managers of the possessions God gives us in a way that brings glory and honor to Him. The truth is, however, that we all have areas in our lives where our stewardship could use some improvement.

Frankly, many of us have misconceptions about what it means to be godly stewards. We think it's all about money. In fact, you may be thinking the book you're holding is just another book about money. But stewardship is bigger than money. In order to be good stewards we must start from the assumption that everything we have in life already belongs to God. We can talk about "our" car all we want, but it really belongs to the Lord. We can talk about "our" house if we want to, but that really belongs to the Lord, too. Even the outfit we're wearing and our hairdo belong to the Lord. Scripture tells us that even we ourselves have been bought with a price (1 Corinthians 6:19–20).

So good stewardship means managing *everything* God has blessed us with, including our time.

"Time?" you might ask. Yes. Some of us waste so much of it. We go home and the phone rings and we answer it.

"What you doing?"

"Nothing."

"What you doing tomorrow?"

"Nothing."

"Girl, what you been doing all week?"

"Nothing."

We ought to be doing something!

In light of the economy and our personal circumstances, we might be struggling to make ends meet despite our best efforts. Yet each of us can become a more effective steward for God by learning and living out these seven basic principles of stewardship:

Principle #1—God Doesn't Need Our Money

Money is not the primary concern. After all, Scripture is clear that God already owns everything. This makes sense, since He created the whole universe, including us!

> *The earth is the LORD'S, and all its fullness, the world and those who dwell therein. For He has founded it upon the seas, and established it upon the waters.* **— Psalm 24:1**

> *...every beast of the forest is Mine, and the cattle on a thousand hills. I know all the birds of the mountains, and the wild beasts of the field are Mine. If I were hungry, I would not tell you; for the world is Mine, and all its fullness.* **— Psalm 50:10-12**

As the Creator and owner of this world, God doesn't need anything. He is self-sufficient, self-existent, and omnipotent.

Principle #2—We Are God's Stewards

God created us to be stewards of His creation. Stewards don't own what is entrusted into their care; they simply manage it on behalf of the owner and for his benefit. God made this clear to Adam and Eve on the day He created them.

> *Then God blessed them, and God said to them, "Be fruitful and multiply; fill the earth and subdue it; have dominion over the fish of the sea, over the birds of the air, and over*

every living thing that moves on the earth." And God said, "See, I have given you every herb that yields seed which is on the face of all the earth, and every tree whose fruit yields seed; to you it shall be for food." — **Genesis 1:28-29**

Then the LORD God took the man and put him in the garden of Eden to tend and keep it. — **Genesis 2:15**

When teaching about the kingdom of heaven, Jesus told this parable that drew from His listeners' familiarity with the owner-steward relationships of their day:

For the kingdom of heaven is like a man traveling to a far country, who called his own servants and delivered his goods to them. And to one he gave five talents, to another two, and to another one, to each according to his own ability; and immediately he went on a journey. Then he who had received the five talents went and traded with them, and made another five talents. And likewise he who had received two gained two more also. But he who had received one went and dug in the ground, and hid his lord's money. After a long time, the lord of those servants came and settled accounts with them.

So he who had received five talents came and brought five other talents, saying, "Lord, you delivered to me five talents; look, I have gained five more talents besides them."

His lord said to him, "Well done, good and faithful servant; you were faithful over a few things, I will make you ruler over many things. Enter into the joy of your lord."

He also who had received two talents came and said, "Lord, you delivered to me two talents; look, I have gained two more talents besides them." His lord said to him,

"Well done, good and faithful servant; you have been faithful over a few things, I will make you ruler over many things. Enter into the joy of your lord."

Then he who had received the one talent came and said, "Lord, I knew you to be a hard man, reaping where you have not sown, and gathering where you have not scattered seed. And I was afraid, and went and hid your talent in the ground. Look, there you have what is yours."

But his lord answered and said to him, "You wicked and lazy servant, you knew that I reap where I have not sown, and gather where I have not scattered seed. So you ought to have deposited my money with the bankers, and at my coming I would have received back my own with interest. Therefore take the talent from him, and give it to him who has ten talents. For to everyone who has, more will be given, and he will have abundance; but from him who does not have, even what he has will be taken away. And cast the unprofitable servant into the outer darkness. There will be weeping and gnashing of teeth." —
Matthew 25:14–30

This parable emphasizes that the role of a steward is like that of a slave who manages his owner's assets for his master's benefit, not his own. The owner expects his stewards to multiply the assets entrusted to them. We must do no less in our management of the resources God has entrusted into our care. They include our time, our talents, and our treasures.

I once read a story about a child and two dollars:

A young girl one day was given two dollars by her mother.

"Darling," said the mother, "one dollar is for church and the other dollar is for candy after church."

> The little girl started on her way to church. But it was a windy day, and before long she tripped and the dollars fell out of her hand. The wind took both bills, but she was able to retrieve one. As the other flew away, she said, "Well, God, there goes your dollar!"[3]

Isn't it interesting that it's always God's dollar that flies away? Have you noticed that when we have to cut, we cut God but nobody else?

Principle #3: We Have a Responsibility to Pay It Forward

In explaining this principle, one pastor wrote: "Although God gives us 'all things richly to enjoy,' nothing is ours. Nothing really belongs to us for God owns everything. We're responsible for how we treat it and what we do with it. While we complain about our rights here on earth, the Bible constantly asks, What about your *responsibilities*? Owners have rights; stewards have responsibilities."

While God has graciously entrusted us, as His stewards, with the care, development, and enjoyment of everything He owns, we have a responsibility to pass on something better to those who are coming behind us.

> *Now therefore, in the sight of all Israel, the assembly of the LORD, and in the hearing of our God, be careful to seek out all the commandments of the LORD your God, that you may possess this good land, and leave it as an inheritance for your children after you forever. — 1 Chronicles 28:8*

Woody Hayes was speaking to graduates at a commencement exercise at Ohio State University, and giving them a challenge for life:

> You can never pay back what this school has done for you," he said. "Even the money you paid didn't completely pay for the quality of education you received at Ohio State University. You can't pay it back. It's an investment that will last you for the rest of your life. But even though you can't pay it back, you can pay it forward."[4]

That concept became a movie, *Pay It Forward*. The idea was to pass along to somebody else the blessing that had been received from the school. Alumni Associations in colleges regularly call upon the alumni to reinvest in others because of the education that they themselves have received. I believe God is calling the church to *pay it forward.*

Principle #4—Material Things Can Be Invested to Reap Eternal Dividends

Material things are not inherently evil, but they are temporary. In fact, the harder we try to hang onto material things, the quicker they seem to disappear. God often reminds us of these realities:

> *Do not overwork to be rich; because of your own understanding, cease! Will you set your eyes on that which is not? For riches certainly make themselves wings; they fly away like an eagle toward heaven. — **Proverbs 23:4-5***

The wise steward realizes he has both an opportunity and a duty to manage God's temporary resources in a way that will increase God's eternal glory. And in His grace, God blesses us and others when we invest temporal resources into things of eternal value.

> *Do not lay up for yourselves treasures on earth, where moth and rust destroy, and where thieves break in and steal. But lay up for yourselves treasures in heaven, where neither moth nor rust destroys, and where thieves do not break in and steal. For where your treasure is, there your heart will be also.* — **Matthew 6:19-21**

Spending Money on What Matters

Transmutation means changing one thing into something else. For example, when we go to the pharmacist we transmute our funds. We exchange money for medicine. The money is turned into something that helps our body. The money itself cannot do the job. We must transmute it into something else to help us.

Money can be transmuted into something else too. It can be used on earth now for the benefit of eternity, so that when we get to heaven, we'll have things there that money cannot buy here.

Twenty-four-year-old Danny Simpson robbed a bank in Ottawa, Canada, at gunpoint and stole six thousand dollars. He was captured shortly afterwards. The real tragedy of this true story is that the weapon he used to rob the bank with was a 1918 .45-caliber semiautomatic Colt worth $100,000. Danny Simpson robbed a bank for

$6,000 with a weapon worth $100,000. Danny's problem was that he didn't know what he had in his hand. If he had known, he probably wouldn't have chosen to be a thief. What he had in his possession would have given him so much more.[5]

If Christians only knew what we had in our possession, we wouldn't be robbing God of His tithes or offerings. If we realized we had God in our possession, we would know we already had everything we needed. When we realize we have God in our possession, we will recognize Him as both our Captain and our Deliverer, one who can do "exceedingly abundantly above all that we ask or think, according to the power that works in us" (Ephesians 3:20).

Principle #5—Stewardship Is about Trust

If we want to improve our stewardship of the blessings God bestows upon us, we need to know it's all about trusting the Lord.

Church-goers who do not tithe or give to God's house are typically those who have an issue with trust, because when we tithe we *have* to trust that the Lord will make a way somehow.

Yet the reason most of us have made it this far is that we've had to trust in the Lord. We've all sent our children to school, and managed to raise them. Some of us just don't know how we made it, but as we look back and reflect, we can truly say the Lord made a way. We simply had to trust Him. That's why the Bible says,

Trust in the LORD with all your heart, and lean not on your own understanding. In all your ways acknowledge Him and He shall direct your paths. — **Proverbs 3:5–6**

So how do we trust Him? Well, first of all we trust Him *entirely*, "with all our heart." It's easy to trust the Lord when we have money in our pocket. I was at the airport waiting for a plane. It was delayed, and people were panicking. Where would their next meal come from? Where would they stay? I wasn't worried because I had some cash in my pocket, and money has a way of easing the situation. But God wants to know how much we trust Him even when we lack money. Can we relax even when we have no cash and are stranded at the airport?

Secondly. The Lord wants us to trust Him *exclusively*. He says in Proverbs, "Lean not on your own understanding." When some of us get in trouble, the first thing we do is get on the phone and ask others for their advice. We look to the thoughts and opinions of others, but the Lord wants us to trust in Him alone. Have you ever been in a situation where you've tried your best to reach someone but nobody would answer the phone? Or you can't recall a phone number? The Lord may put us a position where the only person we can talk to is Him, because He wants us to trust Him exclusively.

Thirdly, He wants us to trust Him *extensively*. That's why the scripture says, "In all your ways acknowledge Him, and He shall direct your paths" (Proverbs 3:6). This means not only on the job but in the home as well. He wants us to trust Him in the church, too, because so often church folk get upset over things that don't really matter. A man named Dr. Richard Carlson once wrote a book called *Don't Sweat the Small Stuff ... and It's All Small Stuff.*[6] It truly is all small stuff. One of the challenges in the church is people getting upset over trivial things. When children have squabbles, five minutes later they're running and skipping around. But adults can still smart over something that happened years ago!

Principle #6—A Good Steward Fears God

If we want to improve our stewardship, we must also *fear* God. The word 'fear' doesn't mean to be afraid; it means to be in awe of God and to respect Him.

> *Do not be wise in your own eyes; fear the LORD and depart from evil.* — ***Proverbs 3:7***

When we fear God, we respect His possessions. When somebody lets us use their car, we try to bring it back in the same or better condition than when we borrowed it. We don't return it empty, with flat tires and scrapes and full of fast food wrappings! If we did, it would show a lack of respect for the owner.

Sadly, a lack of respect has moved over into the church. That's why people come to church any way they want to come. Some of us will spend the whole afternoon getting ready to go to the club. We get our hair done, we wash the car in the morning, and we line up the babysitter. Then we go out and they have to kick us out when the party is over because we aren't ready to go home yet. Then when we finally leave the club scene or hangout spot, we're looking for a midnight special!

We seem to have lost that godly zeal in the church. There we come when we want and leave when we want. We get up in the middle of the sermon and leave, not just to go to the restroom but to go home! We may chat with our friends while the pastor is doing the benediction or even making an altar call. All because we have no fear of the Lord.

When I was growing up, it seemed that we had the fear of the Lord while in the church building. If we slouched in our seat when we came to church, a mother would walk by and tap us on the head.

"Sit up!" she'd tell us. "You are in God's house!" And she'd dare our mama or our daddy to say something.

Now people come however they want, and that's why we have a problem with dress. Our intent is not to be mean, but there ought to be some standards in the house of God and I believe we need to get them back. When we come to God's house we need to enter with a spirit of awe. There ought to be some things we do not say or do in His sanctuary.

Principle #7—A Good Steward Honors God

Stewardship also requires that we *honor* the Lord. That's why the Bible says, "Honor the LORD with your possessions, and with the firstfruits of all your increase" (Proverbs 3:9). Too many of us refuse to honor the Lord with what we have. We are to give to the Lord's work not because He needs our help, but as a way to honor and worship Him. We all know the Lord doesn't need our fifty cents—not in His economy.

Some people want to stop giving when they get mad, and they think they are hurting the church! But they are not. They are dishonoring God because God's Word says to honor Him with their possessions. The Hebrew word for 'honor' is "to be heavy." In other words, if God is heavy, He carries weight. If He means something to us, we will honor Him with our substance, regardless of what other people do. It doesn't depend on whether we like the deacon, or the preacher, or whether somebody in the choir said something about us, or whether somebody didn't call out hello in the parking lot, or whether somebody parked in our parking space or bumped into us and forgot to apologize.

If something happens to cause us to stop giving, we also stop worshiping and fellowshipping. It's not about the pastor or the preachers or the church house, but about the lordship of Christ. We ought to give the Lord the first portion (Scripture calls it the first fruits) of all we receive, and the result of our generosity will be an even greater blessing. In other words, when the Lord blesses us with resources, we give the Lord a portion—ten percent— so that "your barns will be filled with plenty, and your vats will overflow with new wine" (Proverbs 3:10).

I am grateful that we serve a God who is able to keep on giving. I was recently sitting at a table at a birthday party, near a woman was talking about a government shutdown where she worked. She had been placed on furlough and was no longer receiving a steady income. She had to cut back on her spending because she didn't know when her next check would arrive.

My spirit began to leap, not because of the government shutdown or because of her being placed on furlough, but because I knew we both served a God who never shut down. We served a God who never shut down His blessings, His glory, His grace, or His mercy. He just kept on giving and giving and giving.

I don't know about you but I thank God that He continues to give, and if He can, so can I!

Thank God Anyhow

What do we do, however, when circumstances seem to be taking from us more than God is giving?

Baron Friedrich von Hügel, a Roman Catholic philosopher, once wrote a series of letters to his niece. "My dear Gwen," he wrote, "I want to prepare you for life. I want to prepare you not only for life but for illness and for crises and ultimately for death. Live all you can, as complete and full a life as you can find. Do as much as you can for others. Hope for the best but plan for the worst."[7]

In this fast-moving, fun-loving, freedom-loving age in which we live, we're often caught off guard when the worst comes. The despair, dismay, and discouragement we feel today indicates that we don't really believe the worst could happen to us. We see how it happens in the lives of others, but few of us accept that it can happen to us as well.

On Tuesday, September 11, 2001, the United States was caught off guard when terrorists used innocent people to attack America by crashing planes straight into occupied buildings. Today many of us continue to live without adequate back-ups because we don't believe the worst will come. But it does come. Things don't always go according to plan. There are catastrophic circumstances, tumultuous times and perilous predicaments zigzagging across our national and individual horizons. *The worst will come.*

This morning I was talking to a friend who had experienced a string of bad events over the last two weeks. First he had a car accident. Then he was playing basketball when he shouldn't have been. He said his body had told him not to, but his mind had told him he could. When he went in for the lay-up his mind told him, *You can do a turnaround twist and still lay up the basketball.*

His body, on the other hand, said, *That ain't happening today!*

And so the worst happened. For the next several days he couldn't even move.

Yes, friends, the worst can still come. Many of us romanticize life like Charles Dickens, who in *A Tale of Two Cities* declared it was both the best of times and the worst of times. We live in an age of wisdom, and an age of foolishness; the spring of darkness and the winter of despair. But from where I sit, the worst is just around the corner. We only have to look around us.

The rule of the day is to disrespect people in leadership. Schools are filled with young people who believe they should be shooting the place up. Employment is low, healthcare is in bad shape, childcare is poor, and crime is on the rise. I was watching the news last evening and was amazed at how many deaths and robberies we still had, despite all the security measures and cameras. Crime remains high. Even in churches we've reached the point where a woman cannot leave her purse in the pew. We have more security in the church today than we ever did in the past, with cameras all over, but people still dare not leave their personal belongings anywhere. The worst is just around the corner.

So I appreciate the book of Habakkuk. This man, too, was living in the worst of times. In his day the nation of Israel was so defunct and disobedient that the Lord had pronounced judgment on them. God said that Babylon was coming to get them, to take them into captivity. Now, Habakkuk had a real problem! He was upset not only because God's people were being disobedient, but also because God was choosing Babylon to punish them. How could God use a heathen nation to destroy His own people?

It was the worst of times, and Habakkuk was one of those poetic prophets who had a knack of putting words together. In chapter 1 he was asking some desperate questions. But by chapter 2 he could say, "The just shall live by his faith."

He was saying, in effect, "I don't understand what God is doing. The fact is, things are getting worse than I ever thought they could get. But I still have to live by faith in God."

In chapter 3 he began to rejoice. "Even though things are not the way I think they ought to be," he reflected, "and even though things are not the way I think God ought to allow them to be, I am still going to rejoice. Because at the end of the day, God is still in control."

I believe this is a word for today. It's also a word for the church. When I look at this passage of Scripture, when things were looking so bad, I wonder how Habakkuk was still able to worship God and rejoice. I see two things here. In chapter 3, verse 17, he says:

> *Though the flock may be cut off from the fold, and there be no herd in the stalls, yet I will rejoice in the LORD, I will joy in the God of my salvation.* **— Habakkuk 3:17–18**

He could be joyful because he understood that salvation never ceased.

In order for us to rejoice as well, we need to understand what salvation is. In the Old Testament, to be saved was to be delivered from danger. There was danger all around, but Habakkuk understood that God could save him from it. We know God can still deliver us from seen and unseen dangers, but in the New Testament the meaning of the word 'salvation' changes. Now it means to be delivered from sin. While we may not be delivered from danger we absolutely need to be delivered from sin.

When we receive Jesus as our personal Lord and Savior, that's God's salvation. He saves us from the guilt, penalty, power and the presence of sin. When we believe in Christ, we are born again, or "saved." That's why Paul said in Acts 16:31, "Believe on the Lord Jesus Christ, and you will be saved, you and your household" (Acts 16:31).

To be released from the guilt of our sin is the first component of salvation. The second is that we are also being saved from the *grip* of sin through sanctification, or setting ourselves apart for holiness). That's why Paul says in Philippians 2:12–14:

> *Therefore, my beloved, as you have always obeyed, not as in my presence only, but now much more in my absence, work out your own salvation with fear and trembling; for it is God who works in you both to will and to do for His good pleasure. Do all things without complaining or disputing.* — ***Philippians 2:12–14***

You see, when we receive Jesus as our Lord and Savior it does not mean we can no longer make mistakes. We are not going to get saved on Monday and be a perfect saint on Tuesday. We'll still stumble from time to time, and there will be some things in us that the Lord will need to work on. As believers in Christ, we are now going through the process of sanctification—the process of becoming more and more dedicated to God's standard of righteousness (2 Thessalonians 2:13; 1 Corinthians 6:11). As we become more and more dedicated to God's standard of righteousness during the process of sanctification, we also become less and less influenced by the power of sin. Thus, we are in the process of being saved from the *power* of sin. In other words, maturation is taking place, even though we may struggle with sin from time to time.

You know why some people in the church are still murmuring and gossiping? It's because they have not yet been totally delivered from the power of sin! You'd be amazed at some of the things that go on in the house of God, where everyone is supposed to be saved. People say things and think things and do things and pass notes and numbers. Just the other day a friend was telling me how two people were fighting in the sanctuary. This kind of behavior is certainly not tolerated in the sanctuary of God under any circumstance. Yes, we need to be loosened from sin's grip. That is one of the blessings of salvation.

But there's a third component to salvation. We shall be saved not only from the guilt and the power of sin but also from the *presence* of it. That's why Paul wrote to Titus that believers should be "looking for the blessed hope and glorious appearing of our great God and Savior Jesus Christ, who gave Himself for us, that He might redeem us from every lawless deed and purify for Himself His own special people, zealous for good works" (Titus 2:13–14). He added, "Speak these things, exhort, and rebuke with all authority. Let no one despise you" (Titus 2:15).

There will come a time when we will all be saved from the presence of sin in glory. That's why I caution people who hop from one church to the next, looking for the perfect church. They won't ever find it, because the church is made up of *people* and there are no perfect people. If you ever do find the perfect church please don't join it because you'd spoil it.

Why is it important to be saved from the presence of sin? It's because life is always changing. People are fickle. They'll love you on Monday but dislike you on Tuesday. They won't call you on Wednesday, but they'll visit you on Thursday. But the Lord's salvation never ceases. Things may get bad, but nothing and no one can take away our salvation, thank God! The devil can take our car, our house, and even our health, he cannot mess with our salvation! Some people say we can lose our salvation, but how can we lose something that's not even ours? Salvation belongs to the Lord, and He saves us by His own will and power. It's not as if we did something to obtain it. We were on our way to hell and God saved us because of His grace and mercy (Ephesians 2:8–9).

This is why we can be thankful. Not because we speak in tongues, not because we give money to the church, not because we've been a member for a long time, and not because we can quote John 3:16 from memory. It's because of His *grace* that He saved us. Jesus said in John 10:28:

> *And I give eternal life, and they shall never perish; neither shall anyone snatch them out of my hand. My Father who has given them to Me is greater than all, and no one is able to snatch them out of my Father's hand.* — **John 10:28–29**

So we are in the hands of Jesus and we are in the hands of God.

Habakkuk was able to rejoice despite his tough circumstances because salvation never ceases. And he finally understood that his strength would never collapse either. He knew the Lord God was his strength, and when we understand that we can make it too, regardless of what we're going through. We must know in our spirit that God is our strength, whether we're dealing with cancer, or the death of a loved one, or wayward children, or long-term unemployment. We can rejoice because we don't have to do it on our own.

The LORD is my light and my salvation. Whom shall I fear? — ***Psalm 27:1***

David was afraid of nobody. We have a few scaredy-cats in the church who don't see God as their light or their strength. But even David's enemies faltered when they approached him to do him in (Psalm 27:2). They came to get him, but by the time they reached him they stumbled and fell. Why? Because the Lord was his strength.

Though an army may encamp against me, my heart shall not fear. Though war may rise against me, in this I will be confident. — ***Psalm 27:3***

Even when David was on the run, he could say,

One thing I have desired of the LORD, that will I seek: that I may dwell in the house of the LORD all the days of my life, to behold the beauty of the LORD, and to inquire in his temple. — **Psalm 27:4**

We cannot have a spirit of worship and face our enemy unless we understand that the Lord is with us. That's why Paul said, "I can do all things through Christ who strengthens me" (Philippians 4:13).

Somebody has said that God will pick us up, turn us around, and place our feet on solid ground. That's why I've made up in my mind that I'm going to thank God anyhow. Even when my enemies try to destroy me, and my plans don't go the way I want them to go, I'm going to thank God anyhow. Even though I may receive a bad report from the doctor, I'm going to praise God anyhow because He is my strength and my salvation.

Habakkuk said the Lord would make his feet like deer's feet, and make him walk on his high hills (Habakkuk 3:19). Remember how agile and swift deer are. Even though we may be in the valley, the Lord will give us agility and strength to climb the mountains. We might be in the midst of trials and tribulations but the Lord will give us strength to go higher and higher. Isn't He good!

Let us determine, then, that no matter what happens to us, we will thank God anyhow. When things go wrong we will still thank Him. When the sun refuses to shine, when the clouds hover over our heads, and when friend are few, we will thank Him. When the bank account is depleted and we can't see our way through, we will praise His name because He gives us the strength to keep moving.

And we will prepare for the worst to come by remembering that we and all we have are God's, and therefore continuing to be faithful, responsible caretakers of God's blessings. We will continue to give, and give sacrificially—even as He sacrificed for us. "Thank you, Lord," we can say joyfully, "for giving to Me your great salvation so full and free!"

WORKBOOK

Chapter 1 Questions

Question: What does your identity has God's steward mean to you? What responsibilities does it entail?

_____

_____

_____

_____

_____

_____

_____

_____

_____

_____

_____

_____

Question: What material things can you invest to reap eternal dividends—and how?

_____

_____

_____

_____

_____

_____

_____

_____

_____

_____

_____

_____

_____

Question: What level of trust do you have toward God, based on your financial stewardship habits? How, specifically, can you trust Him more fully?

_____

_____

_____

_____

_____

_____

_____

_____

_____

_____

_____

Question: How do you show God that you fear and honor Him? How can you do more to respect and honor Him in your daily life?

_____

_____

_____

_____

_____

_____

_____

_____

_____

_____

_____

_____

Question: Why should you thank God even during difficult circumstances? What trying situations do you need to thank God for today?

_____

_____

_____

_____

_____

_____

_____

_____

_____

_____

_____

_____

Action: Embrace your role as God's steward! Remember that He doesn't need your money, but since you can never fully repay Him for his sacrifice and blessings, you have a responsibility to pay those blessings forward. Invest material things in things that matter, to reap eternal, spiritual dividends. In all of this, trust God to provide for you. Maintain respectful fear of Him and honor Him with the resources He places in your stewardship. Give Him your praise as well—even when things look bad! Never lose faith that He will carry you through and provide for you if you trust in Him.

Chapter 1 Notes

CHAPTER TWO

Tithing God's Way

Biblical stewardship is "the use of God-given resources for the accomplishment of God-given goals." In essence, it defines our purpose in this world as assigned to us by God. It is our divinely-given opportunity to join with God in His worldwide and eternal redemptive movement.

To discover what the Bible says about stewardship, we must start with the very first verse: "In the beginning God created the heavens and the earth" (Genesis 1:1). As the Creator, God has absolute rights of ownership over *everything*.

As Psalm 24:1 reminds us,

*The earth is the LORD'S and all its fullness, the world and those who dwell therein. — **Psalm 24:1***

Even though our name is on our checkbook, on our mortgage, on our credit card and on our retirement account, everything we own really belongs to God. We only need to attend a funeral to realize the truth of this. As the saying goes, "Hearses don't pull U-Hauls!" In other words, we can't take a thing with us when we die.

The last time I went through security at the airport they made me take off my jacket. I noticed the TSA attendant looking at me intently, and began to feel almost flattered. Until she suddenly laughed.

"Sir," she said, "your shirt is buttoned unevenly. The buttons aren't aligned!"

If we don't understand that the Lord has an absolute right of ownership over everything we possess, it's like misaligning the top buttons on our shirt or blouse. Nothing else in the Bible will ever make sense. Only when we grasp it will we fully understand the doctrine of stewardship.

As the apostle Paul put it,

> *For we are God's fellow workers; you are God's field, you are God's building.* — ***1 Corinthians 3:9***

With this understanding we can accurately view and correctly value not only our possessions, but also, and more importantly, life itself.

> *Go therefore, and make disciples of all the nations, baptizing them in the name of the Father, and of the Son, and of the Holy Spirit, teaching them to observe all things that I have commanded you; and, lo, I am with you always, even to the end of the age.* — ***Matthew 28:19–20***

Talents, Time, and Treasure

There are different areas in which we are to be stewards. First, we are stewards of our *talents*. God gives each of us abilities to use for His work (Luke 19:11–27). Every person has the ability to serve Christ in some capacity, and we should use this ability in the ministry of the church.

Secondly, we are to be stewards of our *time*. The Lord promises to bless those who put Him first (Matthew 6:33–34).

Thirdly, we are to be stewards of our *treasury*, including our tithes. One tenth of what we earn belongs to God. So we tithe in order to please the Lord and fulfill His commandments. Abraham tithed four hundred years before the Law was given (Genesis 14:20) and Moses incorporated the tithe into the Law (Leviticus 27:30 tells us "the tithe is the Lord's").

The Scripture teaches us to "Bring the tithes into the storehouse..." (Malachi 3:10) which is none other than our place of worship. During the age of grace this is the local church (1 Corinthians 16:2). The tithe, which Jesus approved (Matthew 23:23), is the only method God has ordained to finance the church and to fund its pastor. If God gave His best for us (John 3:16) we should do no less for Him.

Pastors generally hate to talk about stewardship. In his book *When God Builds a Church*, Bob Russell writes that preachers hate talking about money in the church, perhaps because they are afraid of discouraging the visitors.[8] But the wise stewardship of God's resources is an important part of becoming a healthy church. Because pastors are not talking and teaching about stewardship, people are not giving.

We live in a materialistic culture in which people do battle daily with the god of money. We may be struggling in our finances, hardly able to make ends meet, and yet most preachers are reluctant to even broach the subject.

No matter how we cut it, money is a key issue of life, and we think about it more than we like to admit. We take a job to earn it, and in stores we love to spend it. ABBA even sings about it: "Money, money, money..." We save less of it than we'd like and give less of it than we ought. We actually need *more* sermons on money and stewardship, because the topic is mentioned so often in God's Word. Paul said, "For I have not shunned to declare to you the whole counsel of God" (Acts 20:27). Jesus himself talked more about stewardship than about any other subject.

Pastor John MacArthur once said, "Sixteen out of [thirty-eight] parables of Christ deal with money. More is said in the New Testament about money than [about] heaven and hell combined; five times more is said about money than [about] prayer; and while there are 500 plus verses on both prayer and faith, there are over 2,000 verses dealing with money and possessions."[9]

Hosea 4:6 says, "My people are destroyed for lack of knowledge." We have to be taught about money because it is needed to advance the gospel. We've just been reminded of the Great Commission, in Matthew 28:18– 19. Almost every program or plan for communicating the gospel costs money. How many times have good ideas been turned down and our vision reduced because we've been worried about the cost?

Most people who say "I can't tithe" could tithe, but choose not to. They may be shopping at Macy's on a Walmart budget. Or they may be in the grip of debt. They may be strapped with a house payment that's out of hand; they may owe more on two cars than the cars are worth, with credit cards that are maxed out. It may feel as if a yoke has been strapped to their shoulders, so that they stagger under its burden. This robs them of the joy of giving and results in bondage. Yet we don't want to talk about all this in the church!

Reasons People Don't Give

Casey Graham has suggested reasons why people might not be giving to the church.[10] The first is that they don't feel needed. Because we don't want to look like a second-rate church, we try to make our churches look professional and successful. People park the cars in the parking lot, we have nice signs, and we have great children's workers. We're trained to create a culture where everything feels "done" and people feel welcomed more than they feel needed. However, while we project the idea that everything is okay, the church may be struggling to stay afloat financially.

Yet people *want* to be needed. They are attracted to needs. As James the apostle said, "[You] do not have because you do not ask…" (James 4:2).

Secondly, people don't *understand*. We assume that because it's clear to us, it's also clear to them. If people only had a clear picture of where the church was headed, we could solve most of our funding issues. People need vision and clarity about the future more than we think they do.

According to Casey Graham, "People's giving rarely increases unless you give them something to stretch for." It is a fact that when a church has three or four objectives that they want to accomplish through their operational budget, and they highlight these to the congregation and ask specifically for support, people start giving!

Proverbs 29:18 says, "Where there is no revelation, the people cast off restraint. But happy is he who keeps the law."

Once a mother wanted to teach her daughter a moral lesson, so she gave her daughter both a quarter and a dollar for church:

> "Put whichever one you want in the collection plate and keep the other for yourself," she told the girl.
>
> When they were coming out of church, the mother asked her daughter which amount she had given.
>
> "Well," said the little girl, "I was going to give the dollar, but just before the collection the man in the pulpit said that we should all be cheerful givers. I knew I'd be a lot more cheerful if I gave the quarter, so I did."[11]

Thirdly, people may feel as if the church wants something *from* them, but not *for* them. If the only time we talk about money is when we need it, people get nervous when we start to raise the subject.

A Vision of Stewardship

When we go to a doctor for our annual check-up, he or she will often begin to poke, prod, and press various places, all the while asking, "Does this hurt? How about this?"

If we cry out in pain, one of two things has happened. Either the doctor has pushed too hard, without the right sensitivity, or, more likely, there's something wrong. Then the doctor will say, "We'd better do some more tests and send you to a specialist. It's not supposed to hurt there!"

When pastors preach on financial stewardship, certain members cry out in discomfort, criticizing both the message and the messenger. Either the pastor has pushed too hard, or perhaps something is wrong. In that case we can say, "My friends, we're in need of the Great Physician, because it's not supposed to hurt there!"

By the same token, when the leaders are lost, how can we expect the followers to be on the right track?

As a train was about to leave a large railroad station, the conductors began to take tickets. Looking at the ticket of the first passenger he remarked, "Friend, I think you're on the wrong train."

"But the ticket agent told me this was my train," replied the man.

> After a little while another conductor came and said, "Friend, I think you're on the wrong train!"
>
> "But the ticket agent told me this was my train!" protested the passenger.
>
> After a little discussion, the two conductors decided to check with the ticket agent. Before long, it became clear that both conductors were on the wrong train![12]

Church leaders and members alike need a vision. A church's vision statement is sometimes called a picture of that church in the future. Our vision statement is our inspiration, the framework for all our strategic planning. It answers the question, "Where do we want to go?" A vision articulates our dreams and hopes for our church and ministry, reminding us of what we're trying to build.

Stewardship requires a vision and a faith commitment made to God, not to a particular church. This commitment begins with the giving of ourselves totally and completely to Jesus Christ as our Savior and Lord. Out of this commitment then flows the awesome desire to give to God a tithe (or tenth) of everything we own. This is done not out of a sense of duty or guilt, but from a heart of gratitude for the grace and love God has poured into our lives. Stewardship, then, is our response to God's grace and forgiveness, and to the love shown to us in Jesus Christ.

Filling the Storehouse

Malachi was the last of the prophets. The times in which he lived—about four hundred years before

Christ—were remarkably similar to our own. The house of the Lord was being robbed of its glory and its tithes and offerings. God's chosen people were intermarrying with the pagan nations around them and therefore failing to fulfill their rightful responsibilities. So Malachi's message was one of exposure, rebuke, and challenge. Right at the heart of his prophecy, however, this faithful preacher lays down the basis for blessings. And he has the audacity to talk about money!

"Bring all the tithes into the storehouse," he says (Malachi 3:10). Not to your house or my house. Not to the dope dealer's house or the casino house or the club house or the vacation house, but to the storehouse. From the time of Hezekiah (2 Chronicles 31:11) a storehouse had been built in the sanctuary for depositing the tithes and offerings of the people. God stated clearly that all the tithes and offerings of the people were to be brought to one place. In fact, if a man lived too far away to carry his corn, wine, or the firstborn of his herds and flocks, he was instructed to turn his goods into money in order that he might "go to the place where which the LORD your God chooses" (Deuteronomy 14:21).

The New Testament counterpart of this principle is that church members should give their tithes to the local church. The money brought in might and should meet some needs beyond the church's walls, but the responsibility to bring all the tithes to the local church is revealed in the Old Testament and affirmed in the New. So "storehouse tithing," means bringing our tithes to the place where our membership is established, our spiritual life is nourished, and our church privileges are enjoyed. If we give elsewhere, it should be over and above this.

Tithing is 400 years older than the law. Abraham gave a tenth to God through Melchizedek, the king-priest (Genesis 14:18–20). According to the seventh chapter of Hebrews, Melchizedek was a type of Christ in His resurrection. Melchizedek gave Abraham bread and wine, symbols of service; and Abraham acknowledged his indebtedness to God by giving Melchizedek tithes of all his spoils. In other words, tithing is the scriptural way of saying thank you to God for all He has done for us.

In his book *The Grace of Giving*, Stephen Olford uses this illustration:

> I go to a home where there is a little girl, five or six years old, and give her a box of chocolates. She at once disappears, and when she returns her lips and fingers are covered with chocolate and she wants more! In another home, however, the box is opened at once, and brought to me.
>
> "You have the first one," the little girl says.
>
> "Oh, no!" I say, "they are for you."
>
> "But you brought them to me," she insists. "Do please have the first one."
>
> Helping myself I say, "Thank you, dear."
>
> Which child has the warmest place in my affections, and which is more likely to get another box of chocolates? The tithe is the first chocolate handed back to God. For some, it will be one-tenth of the total income; for others, it will be more. But never will it be less.[13]

In addition to the tithes are the *offerings*. This word means the freewill giving which is over and above the basic tithe. The Bible teaches that God demands the tithes, whereas He deserves the offerings. He demands the tithes because such giving is for our own good and blessing. He deserves the offerings, because such an overflow from our heart satisfies His heart.

In his book *The Grace of Giving*, Stephen Olford writes of a pastor who came up with an idea on how to get his church to give:

> He announced one Sunday that he had made a new offering box for the weekly collection, one that was designed to encourage people to become better stewards of their money.
>
> "This new box," he explained, "has some interesting features. When you drop in a check or paper money in large amounts, the box makes no sound at all. Put a quarter in and it tinkles like a bell. A dime blows a whistle, and a penny fires a shot. When you put in nothing, the box takes your picture."[14]

"Bring all the tithes into the storehouse, that there may be food in my house."

The children of Israel were supposed to bring all their tithes directly to God's house and hand them over to the Levites and the priest. The Levites and priest were to be supported by these tithes while they took care of the temple, of the worship, and of the spiritual needs of the people. The tithes and offerings were the only means by which the Levites and priests lived, since they had no inheritance of their own (Numbers 18:20–32). In the same way, God has ordained that the church should function by means of the tithes and offerings of His believing people (1 Corinthians 9:1–14).

Supporting the Pastor

Any discussion of stewardship would be incomplete if we did not consider our stewardship to the *pastor*, a theme that recurs throughout the Bible.

In Old Testament times, the priests were to receive "all the tithes in Israel as an inheritance in return for the work which they perform, the work of the tabernacle of meeting" (Numbers 18:21). Failure of the children of Israel to keep this command was regarded as robbing God himself. Hence Jehovah's solemn words in Malachi's day: "You are cursed with a curse, for you have robbed me…" (Malachi 3:9).

In the New Testament the teaching concerning the support of the pastor is just as clear. Sending forth His disciples for their first evangelistic crusade, the Lord said, "Provide neither gold nor silver nor copper in your money belts, nor bag for your journey, nor two tunics, nor sandals, nor staffs; for a worker is worthy of his food" (Matthew10:9–10).

Ministerial support in most of our modern churches is on the basis of a salary and/or love offering. How this salary is determined largely depends on the spiritual level of the congregation. Some church members think it's cool to keep their pastor humble and poor, but the Scripture doesn't support this view.

In apostolic times, Paul made it abundantly clear that "the Lord commanded that those who preached the gospel should live from the gospel" (1 Corinthians 9:14). Writing to Timothy, Paul reminded this young pastor of the scriptural teaching that they should "not muzzle an ox while it treads out the grain" and that the laborer was "worthy of his wages" (1 Timothy 5:18).

"Let him who is taught the word share in *all good things* with him who teaches" (Galatians 6:6). This is one of the clearest statements in the Bible regarding ministerial support. Everybody who profits from true evangelical preaching by the pastor should pay close attention to what the spirit of the Lord is saying.

Paul said in 1 Timothy 5:17, "Let the elders who rule well be counted worthy of *double honor*, especially they who labor in the word and doctrine." The believers were obligated to recognize those who were appointed and anointed to minister the Word of God.

The early church leaders instituted an organized system of instruction that demanded not only the recognition, but also the compensation of the preachers of God's Word. From the beginning the apostles warned the church, "It is not desirable that we should leave the word of God and serve tables ... but we will give ourselves continually to prayer and to the ministry of the word" (Acts 6:2, 4).

God never intended for His preachers to be poor while those who were enriched by their ministry lived as princes, but the idea that a pastor should be content to live in poverty has somehow taken hold in Christian thought. Because Jesus was born in a stable and lived as a poor man, some church folk believe their pastor should also live that way.

The greatest crime in history was the failure of people to recognize the ministry of Jesus and to show this by receiving Him into their hearts and homes and giving Him of their best. Instead, it is recorded that "He came to His own, and His own did not receive Him" (John 1:11). What they did to the Master, some people still try to do to the pastor today! A minister has the right to expect a standard of living that is commensurate with his high and holy vocation. The pastor is worthy of "double honor" because he is a leader both privately and publicly. He is called to be a comforter, a healer, a worshiper, a writer, a reconciler, an administrator, an overseer, a teacher, a preacher, and a friend. None of this can be done without sufficient ministerial support.

Giving Till It Feels Good

A well-known pastor tells a story about hearing an announcement in a morning service that it was time to receive the missionary offering. Then he heard someone sitting behind him saying, "Good. Here's my chance to get rid of some of these pennies."[15]

Most of us have heard the expression, "Give till it hurts." I have a problem with that expression, however, because mostly we give from our excess. Most of us give at a level where we don't miss very much. We donate our spare change.

There are still a lot of Christians getting rid of their pennies, giving to God what essentially costs them little or nothing. This attitude is seen not only in terms of monetary offerings. We give away our clothes with the same mentality. We sometimes discard clothes that are good but a little out of style—a little too old or small. Some of us give our service in the same spirit. We will accept only those responsibilities that we can perform in our spare time. We don't want to do anything that will cost us a lot of energy and time.

But there is another level of giving—it's called *sacrificial* giving. People really know when they have given at this level because typically it will cost them sacrificially. They will have to sacrifice time, talent, and treasure (money). At this level we give not from our reserve but from our operating capital. At this level it may be painful, but the reason I have the problem with the expression "Give until it hurts" is that it doesn't take much giving for most of us to hurt. Some of us are hurting after we give twenty-five or thirty cents! Some of us hurt after we give ten dollars, and for some just the mention of giving makes us hurt!

The preacher stands up and talks about giving a tithe or an offering and we say, "There he goes again, always talking about money." But as we mentioned in the introduction to this book, we don't accuse the grocery store or the service station or the restaurant of always wanting our money. We hand over the cash because they have what we want and we want what they have.

It hurts so much for some of us to give that we will let good food spoil in our refrigerator rather than give it away to somebody who could use it. And some sisters have shoes in the closet for months with the tag still on them because it hurts to give them away! Some of us have more cars than we can even drive!

Our goal should not be to give until it hurts but to give until it feels good. That's why I like the passage in 2 Corinthians 9 where Paul talks about the grace of giving. In the first five verses, Paul brags on the Corinthians' past enthusiasm to collect an offering for the saints at Jerusalem. These were a people who were accustomed to giving, because they understood it required *grace* to give. A stingy Christian is an oxymoron because born-again believers understand that the greatest gift of all was given to us in the person of Jesus Christ when He bled and died on the cross for our sins. If God gave His only begotten Son, who are we as believers to be miserly towards others?

So Paul commended the church members at Corinth for their gracious giving and urged them to complete this task. They didn't have to give but they knew that the love of God was so great that the least they could do was to support the ministry of their Lord and Savior. Paul reminded them of the principle of giving and how to participate in it. Based on what he had already praised them for, he urged each member to give as he purposed in his heart. They were not to be grudging, because God loved "a cheerful" giver (2 Corinthians 9:7). The Greek word translated 'cheerful' means 'hilarious.' So we ought to give with a measure of enthusiasm. Indeed, God wants us to be excited! Too many people walk around with frowns on their faces as if they have been sucking all day on lemons.

Many of us read this passage without properly understanding it. So in order for us to give until it feels good, let us be clear what Paul said. He did not say, "Let every man give according to the way his neighbor purposes." Our giving is not to be based on what others do. We are to give as we *purpose in our heart.* The problem with many of us is that we compare our giving to that of our neighbor. We look at those who seem to be more blessed than us, and because we can't give us much as they do, we think our own giving is less important. We need to be careful because the enemy is keen to discourage us. Scripture says he "walks about like a roaring lion, seeking whom he may devour" (1 Peter 5:8). He wants to distract us from giving to the ministry of God.

Did you hear about the preacher and his wife who were newly-weds? They were on a tight budget, but the preacher's wife went shopping and came home with this beautiful red dress.

Her husband said, "Baby, don't you know we're not supposed to be spending that kind of money?"

She said, "Well baby, the devil made me do it."

He said, "You've got to tell that devil to get behind you."

She said, "I told him to get behind me and he said you sure look good from back here, too!"

We must be careful not to let the devil in because he will make us think our gift is cheap, and then when the opportunity comes we will keep it in our pockets and say, "They won't even miss it!"

Let me tell you, every penny, every nickel, every dime makes a difference. We think when it comes to church that a penny is not going to count. Well, when you pull up at McDonald's and find yourself two cents short of a Happy Meal, I'll bet you start looking in the ashtray and in the console on the floor to scrape up a couple of cents. Every penny helps!

One of the areas in which I believe the church has fallen short is that we have belittled small gifts to God. Remember when Jesus wanted to feed five thousand and a little boy brought Him a lunch of two fish and five barley loaves? Somebody said, "What is that among so many?" But Jesus accepted the gift, gave thanks for it, distributed it and fed the multitudes with it. Then they had leftovers!

When a woman anointed Jesus with an alabaster bottle of expensive ointment, some belittled her gift and called it a waste. But Jesus accepted that gift. In fact, He declared that whenever the gospel would be preached, her gift would be mentioned. Remember the widow with the two mites? Jesus declared that because she had given her all she had, she had given more than all the rest. Jesus would never disparage our gift, and we cannot allow the devil or our neighbor to belittle it either.

Giving feels good because it is based upon what you have. The reason the church is in the shape it's in today, around the country, is that Christians have forgotten how to ante up. I know of churches who have sponsored building programs by bringing coins to the church, because they understood that every penny adds up. From time to time I go to a relative's house. This particular relative seems to always corner me, wanting a dollar and some change. While I do not mind giving them money from time to time, I have found cash in their home just by looking on the floor! I see a dime here, a nickel there, just like we do when we look in the ashtray of the car. I remember thinking once, "The money for which they are asking me is already within their grasp—all they have to do is look on the floor."

Tithing feels good because it's not based on any predetermined amount. So we ought to thank God for the tithe. I am actively involved with a few community organizations and with some organizations you have to pay specific dues before you can join. But the church is not like that. Tithing is based on what we have. If my income is $100 and I give $10 or if my allowance is fifty cents and I give a nickel, then I have given as much, proportionately, as the person with an income of $1000 who puts in $100. I need not feel inferior because of my $10 or my nickel. And the person who gives the $100 has no right to feel superior to the person has given less, based on his income, than I have given based on mine.

A Resurrection Life

While God blesses those who are good stewards, He "curses" those who rob Him. To hold back what is due to God is nothing short of theft. The sin of Ananias and Sapphira was that they robbed God, and the penalty was death (Acts 5). Every time we withhold what rightfully belongs to the Lord, we commit robbery.

Isn't it amazing how we can sit in church and criticize people who hang out at the club, who walk the streets at night, and who socialize with bedfellows like Jim Beam, Jack Daniels, Johnny Walker, and Mr. Boston? But we say nothing about members of the church who attend week after week and rob God!

God insists that until we give to Him what is rightfully His, there will be no fullness of blessing in His house. On the other hand, if these conditions are faithfully met, then we'll experience something amazing.

"'[And] try me now in this,' says the LORD of hosts, 'if I will not open for you the windows of heaven and pour out for you such blessing that there will not be room enough to receive it'" (Malachi 3:10). The original Hebrew language describing the extent of God's blessing literally, means "until there is sufficiency," or "until there is no more need."

That's why Paul said, "And my God shall supply all your need according to His riches in glory by Christ Jesus" (Philippians 4:19). The people had disobeyed God by robbing Him of their tithes and offerings. Actually, when God's people are not faithful in their giving, they rob not only God, but also themselves.

God also promises He will "rebuke the devourer" for our sake. The locusts had eaten the crops, and mildew had destroyed what was left. These physical pests and destroying elements had represented the enemies of God's people. Today they symbolize the forces of Satan that come against the church. God is saying "When the enemy comes in like a flood, I will lift up a standard!"

"'And all nations will call you blessed, for you will be a delightful land,' says the LORD of hosts" (Malachi 3:12). Here, Malachi says that when the surrounding nations see the prosperity that follows true giving to God, they will come to the right conclusion that the Lord is blessing the people. The world is generally unimpressed by the church's witness today, but when it sees us doing what God has called to do, it can only say, "What a mighty God they serve!"

So how do we make this happen? We need leaders and congregation members alike to understand the stewardship vision. What if every person in the church understood the Malachi passage and carried it out? Think about the impact it would have on the church's vision!

The First Epistle to the Corinthians begins with the affirmation that "God is faithful, by whom we are called into the fellowship of His Son, Jesus Christ our Lord" (1 Corinthians 1:9). This theme is then developed with accompanying words of correction and instruction to show that there pulsates throughout the whole church of Christ one common resurrection life by the indwelling presence of the Holy Spirit.

The occasion of this instruction in giving was that there was a crisis in the church at Jerusalem. Because of persecution and opposition, many believers had suffered loss. Some had lost their physical goods, some had lost their homes, and some had even lost their livelihood. Paul felt it was his duty to provide financial assistance for such poverty-stricken saints in the mother church.

The letter concludes with the words, "Therefore, my beloved brethren, be steadfast, immovable, always abounding in the work of the Lord, knowing that your labor is not in vain ... Now concerning the collection for the saints ... On the first day of the week let each one of you lay something aside, storing up as he may prosper..." (1 Corinthians 15:58–16:2).

In the original Greek, there was no break between the fifteenth and sixteenth chapters. Paul found no difficulty in moving from the theological heights of chapter 15 to the practical depths of chapter 16 because he knew that a shared resurrection life in Christ was a serving life. The Lord Jesus gave himself in death and resurrection, not in order to save us from sacrifice, but rather to teach us how to give ourselves and our substance in continual sacrifice.

Abiding Principles of Giving

Embedded in Paul's admonition were principles that would abide for all time: giving to God with *regularity*, giving out of personal *responsibility*, and giving in *reciprocity*.

On the first day of the week let each one of you lay something aside, storing up as he may prosper, that there be no collections when I come. — *1 Corinthians 16:2*

Orderliness and regularity are two of the characteristics of our God. We see this in nature as well as in the church. The word to His believing people is, "Let all things be done decently and in order" (1

Corinthians 14:40). So the first day of the week is a day not only of worship and service but also of *giving* when we come to settle our account with the Lord.

Because giving was such an honor, Paul wanted the collections to be made *before* his arrival in Corinth. He did not want the members' giving to depend upon his being there.

"Let every one of you lay something aside" means that no member was excluded. The message was specific and the application inescapable. Old and young, rich and poor, everybody must be involved in this matter of Christian giving. Remember that Jesus, our Lord commended the widow's mite to teach us that nobody was too poor to give:

> On his tenth birthday a sensitive boy received ten shiny silver dollars from an uncle.
>
> The child was very appreciative and immediately sat down on the floor, spreading the coins before Him. Then he planned how to use the money.
>
> He set aside the first dollar saying, "This one is for Jesus."
>
> He then went on to decide what to do with the second, and so on until he came to the last dollar. "This one is for Jesus," he said.
>
> The boy's mother interrupted, "But I thought you gave the *first* dollar to Jesus."
>
> "I did," the boy replied. "The first one really belongs to Him, but this one is a gift to Jesus from me."[16]

Acts 20:35 reminds us that Jesus said it was more blessed to give than to receive.

This whole matter of giving to God involves thought, time, and planning. How we come to worship without the preparation and consecration of gifts ought to put some of us to shame. Laying something aside, or "storing up" is an activity of disciplined giving that takes place before the money is brought to the church.

Reciprocity is the principle of taking and giving, and Paul teaches that we cannot always be taking without giving. If we have any conscience at all, we are bound to reciprocate by giving back, in some measure, what the Lord has blessed us with.

Consider what we have received from God: first of all we have had physical blessings such as health, strength, vitality, talents, time and treasury. "for in Him we live and move and have our being..." (Acts 17:28). Secondly we have received spiritual blessings. He has blessed us "with every spiritual blessing ... in Christ" (Ephesians 1:3). We are adopted as sons and daughters, accepted in the beloved, a "chosen generation, a royal priesthood, a holy nation and His special people" (1 Peter 2:9).

Most importantly, we have experienced the forgiveness of sin. We were bought with a price and have redemption through His blood. We have everlasting life, and we know the mystery of his will. We have an inheritance and are sealed with His Spirit (Ephesians 1:11–14).

All our giving reflects how much we appreciate God's prospering hand upon us. Before we decide what we should return to God, it is good to remember that the collection which Paul requested was over and above the normal giving of the church at Corinth. Of the six or more words that were used in the New Testament to describe monetary gifts to God, the apostle used a special term in our text which meant an "extra collection." This was in addition to the tithe. Note, further, that Paul did not state the exact amount they were to give to God, but left the matter open to each yielded believer.

Instructed Christians, in the apostles' day, would know that under the law the Jew was bound to give one-tenth of his income to God. Then, of course, there were freewill offerings, trespass offerings, and costly journeys to the temple. It has been estimated that the aggregate of religious gifts among the Jews in olden times could not have been less than one-fifth of each man's income.

So the New Testament leaves the matter open for us to act in proportion to the prospering of God. But if the Old Testament saints, under the law, could give amounts of this kind, can we, under grace, give God any less? This type of giving will cost us, because we must give to keep the work of God alive in our churches.

In his book *The Royal Route to Heaven*, Dr. Alan Redpath writes of a Christian woman who said this to a friend:

"Our church costs too much. They're always asking for money!"

Her friend replied with a story. "Some time ago a little boy was born in our home. He cost (us) a lot of money from the very beginning: he had a big appetite, he needed clothes, medicine, toys, and even a puppy. Then he went to school, and that cost a lot more. Later he went to college, and then he began dating, and that cost a small fortune! But in his senior year at college he died, and since the funeral, he hasn't cost us a penny. Which situation would you rather have?"

After a long pause the friend continued, "As long as this church lives, it will cost us something. When it dies because of lack of support, it won't cost us anything."[17]

Let us remember that giving is the price of keeping our church alive. And she must live if the Savior is to be glorified, the world is to be evangelized, and the devil is to be horrified.

Unseen Resources

The person who gives much is simply following Scripture, for the Bible says that to whom much is given much is required (Luke 12:48). So before we complain about having to give a lot, maybe we ought to think about how much we have received. Remember, each of us should give what we have decided in our heart to give, not reluctantly or under compulsion, "for God loves a cheerful giver."

He did not say that each of us should give according to our bills and expenses. Trying to make a decision to tithe or give based on our bills or obligations is like trying to walk on water by looking at the wind and the waves. We can't do it. Peter discovered that about two thousand years ago. The only way we can walk on water in the midst of the storm is to keep our eyes on Jesus. As soon as Peter took his eyes off the Lord, the only way he could go was down. Looking at Jesus did not make the wind subside or the raging waters calm, but it did help Peter stay firm despite everything. It helped him keep a proper focus so that even in the midst of the storm he wouldn't sink. If we just looked at our bills and obligations, most of us wouldn't tithe at all. A number of us are already one paycheck away from sinking. We just need one phone call to say there are accounting problems at work and that they are going to defer our paycheck until next month, and we're in deep trouble.

When we tithe, it doesn't mean we've forgotten our financial difficulties. We haven't forgotten about our house loan, our car loan, the grocery bill, the college tuition for our children or even the utilities. When we tithe, it doesn't mean our bills will miraculously disappear. Rather, we understand that there is another power at work in the midst of the storms of life. Tithers understand that the winds and the waves obey God's will. They understand that the Lord is able to make a way out of no way. Even though they might not know what tomorrow holds, they know who holds tomorrow.

We may not know how turbulent the seas may become, but we know that if we keep our eye on Jesus, we will not sink. We may bend but we won't break. We may trip but we won't fall. We may go down but we'll ultimately get back up again. Remember that clown toy that bobs back up when you knock it down? It bounces back up because the manufacturer put something inside it that makes it behave like that. When we became born-again believers, something was put inside of us that enables us get up again even after being battered by life's storms.

Some of us have had our backs against the wall. Some of us have been bankrupt. We've lost a home or a car and we've had bad credit. But look at us now! We're still here. We understand that there's another power at work. We have unseen resources.

I was thinking about my mother Annie-Mae. How in the world did she, who never finished high school, raise seven kids? We lived most of our lives in government housing and never owned a car or a home, but I never once went to bed hungry, or without a roof over my head. Every day, I went to school. I didn't have new clothes but the ones I had were clean and pressed. Others have been in the same situation. We've been in circumstances where others have written us off, but look at us now! We're still here, only because we have unseen resources.

A woman was walking back to her dorm from the college library after staying there too late. A rapist was known to be lurking on the campus, and as the woman walked, she began to pray, "The Lord is my shepherd; I shall not want." She kept praying until she got down to "Yea, though I walk through the valley of the shadow of death I will fear no evil, for thou art with me." As she was walking to her dorm, a man walked up to her. He looked at her with wide eyes and then asked her for a light for his cigarette. She said, "Well, sir, I don't smoke and I don't have a light," and kept walking. She got to her dorm room and turned on the TV. There was a news alert announcing that the serial rapist had been captured on campus. They showed his picture.

She looked at him.

"I know him!" she said. "That's the man who walked up to me and asked me for a light."

She called the police station and told a detective she had seen the man.

"This man asked me for light," she said. "But I have a question, sir. Why didn't he touch me? I was walking alone." She went down to the police station and wanted to talk to the man but the detective said there was no way they could let her do that.

"Just tell me what you want," said the detective, "and I will go and ask him."

About fifteen minutes later he came back.

"Well, what did he say?" she asked.

"He said he saw you, but you had somebody with you."

"What do you mean? I didn't have anybody with me."

"Oh yes, you had somebody standing behind you. He said the man had on a long white robe and his eyes were blazing, as if on fire. He said his feet and his hands were the color of bronze, and his hair was white like wool. And in his hand he had a sharp sword!"

Brothers and sisters, we have unseen resources, God is with us! I don't know about you, but that's why I give. I know we sometimes think our service goes unrecognized and unnoticed and unappreciated, but we keep on giving because we are children of God and God is with us. He'll walk with us, talk with us, and let us know everything is going to be all right. We just need to put our hand in His hand, trust in Him with all our heart, and lean not on our own understanding—for if in all our ways we acknowledge Him, He will direct our paths (Proverbs 3:5–6).

WORKBOOK

Chapter 2 Questions

Question: How much of your treasure do you give to God, and to others for His sake? Do you give enough—and how do you know? Are you tithing regularly, responsibly, and reciprocally? Do you give until it feels good?

_____

_____

_____

_____

_____

_____

_____

_____

_____

_____

_____

Question: What do you give to God and the church out of your talents and time? What more can (and should) you give of yourself in these respects?

_____

_____

_____

_____

_____

_____

_____

_____

_____

_____

_____

_____

Question: What is your attitude in giving? Are you a cheerful and joyful giver? How might your attitude in giving require adjustment?

_____

_____

_____

_____

_____

_____

_____

_____

_____

_____

_____

_____

Question: What vision of stewardship guides you personally? What is your church's vision of stewardship? Are you living up to it?

_____

_____

_____

_____

_____

_____

_____

_____

_____

_____

_____

_____

Question: What unseen resources has God provided you, in the past or present?

_____

_____

_____

_____

_____

_____

_____

_____

_____

_____

_____

_____

Action: Give your talents, time, and treasure for godly goals. Maintain a godly vision, for yourself and for your church, that involves stewardship and giving as an extension of your devotion to the Lord. Don't offer excuses or try to justify stinginess, and don't rob God by clinging to material possessions! Rather, tithe according to biblical principles—according to what you have, and no less than ten percent, trusting God's guidance for giving. Fill the storehouse of the local church and support your pastor, remembering that Jesus was a pastor too. Live a resurrection life, giving regularly out of responsibility and reciprocity. Don't merely give till it hurts—give till it feels good! Be a cheerful giver, remembering that God provides for His people with resources both seen and unseen.

Chapter 2 Notes

CHAPTER THREE

Living Sacrifice

I see a major shift in the local church. It's a shift that transcends every denomination, every city, every state, and every convention. We're living at a time when more and more believers know less and less about God, when people no longer see the need for Bible study, or Sunday school, or vacation Bible school.

More and more people know less and less about God or about His will for their lives. I cannot tell you how many times over the years I've talked to people who have a relationship with the Lord but who do not know God's will for their life. But here's the kicker: God *wants* us to know His will for our life, and He wants us to know His Word.

Some believers are walking around still trying to figure out where they fit, in the body of Christ. Many of us have been in church for a long time—we may have been reared in it—and we ought to know what the Lord would have us do. God works through knowledge. There would be less division in the church, and less depression, if only we knew the things God wants us to know.

The Bible tells us in Exodus 19:3:

> *And Moses went up to God and the* LORD *called to him from the mountain, saying, "Thus you shall say to the house of Jacob, and tell the children of Israel..."* —
> **Exodus 19:3**

In other words, "Moses, come here! I've got something to say to you and what I say to you I want you to tell my chosen people."

God wanted to remind the people that they had seen with their own eyes what He did to the Egyptians, and how He bore them on eagles' wings and brought them to himself.

I believe this passage of Scripture has an important message for us. God didn't call Moses up on Mount Sinai just to have a conversation. He had something He wanted Moses to pass on to the people of God. Remember, the children of Israel had recently been brought out of the slavery they'd been in for more than four hundred years. They were about to be prepared, through the wilderness, to enter into God's promised land, a land that was flowing with milk and honey. God needed them to get this message, because if they didn't, they wouldn't enter His promises.

The reason so many of us in the body of Christ today —even those who have been Christians for ages—do not experience the promises of God is that we haven't yet got the memo. And we haven't got it because there is too much division in the church. If we'd gotten the message we'd be in a place of love and unity. The message is this: "Beloved, I want you to know that I brought you out on the wings of an eagle. And I didn't just bring you out—I brought you to *myself*!"

When God brought each of us out of darkness into His marvelous light, He brought us not to a building but to a Person. When He delivered us, He delivered us to *himself*. He bought us with a price, and therefore we no longer own ourselves (I Corinthians 6:19–20). Belonging to the Lord means we do not get to do what we want to do. Rather, we do what *He* wants us to do. If we don't get that message, our marriage, our children, and our job will not go well.

We cannot go into a marriage thinking we own ourselves. In the Bible Paul tells us our body no longer belongs to us, but to our mate. The point is, we no longer belong to ourselves (1 Corinthians 7:4). God brought us out of darkness to himself. He says, "I have delivered you and now I want you to *know me*."

Paul wrote in Philippians 3:10 of his motivations for submitting all earthly possessions and desires to Christ: "…that I may know Him and the power of His resurrection, and the fellowship of His sufferings, being conformed to His death, if, by any means, I may attain to the resurrection from the dead" (Philippians 3:10–11).

We know Paul had a salvation experience on the road to Damascus, but here he tells us that his great goal in life is to *get to know the Lord*. That should be our goal, too. Because once we know the Lord and His will for our life, we will be able to affirm Paul's words in Philippians

2:13: "…it is God who works in you both to will and to do for His good pleasure" (Philippians 2:13).

When we get that message, there are three things we will pick up. The first is the need to *teach*, the second thing is the need to *tithe*, and the third is the need to *toss*.

First, we are to *teach*. Every challenge in the church and in life is connected to teaching. The problem is, many of us do not like being taught. It seems as if too many Christians want to play games with God's Word and pick and choose what they want to be taught. The time for playing church is far past. God wants us to come to church and be taught His Word. The Lord Jesus told us, "Go therefore and make disciples of all nations, baptizing them in the name of the Father and of the Son and of the Holy Spirit, *teaching* them to observe all things I have commanded…" (Matthew 28:19).

Secondly we need to *tithe*. I thought about this when I went to a restaurant the other day with my family and we were discussing how we would tip. They knew the standard was ten percent, and if the food was particularly good, fifteen. And if the service was outstanding, twenty.

Some of us even decide how deep a relationship is going to go, based on how our date is tipping. We watch, and if they give a five percent tip we say, "No, they're cheap!"

But when that same group goes to church, they seem to get amnesia. They tip the equivalent of a tithe or better when they go to a restaurant, but when it comes to tithing to God, they suddenly get extremely theological.

"Do I tithe on the gross or on the net?" we ask. Or, "That's Old Testament, that's the law, but aren't we in the New Testament under grace?"

God wants us to tithe. He tells us to "Bring all of the tithes into the storehouse, that there may be food in My house…" (Malachi 3:10). This is not our house. It's *His*.

Thirdly, we are to *toss*. Peter tells us to "[cast] all your care upon Him, for H*e cares for you* (1 Peter 5:7). God says, "I brought you out, and I want you to come to me. Now I want you to bring everything, including your problems, your trials and your tribulations, and cast them on me, because I care."

Friends don't mind when we cast our cares on them. We ought to thank God for some of our problems because He will use adversity to let us know who our real friends are.

Finally, we need to understand that there is a *method* in this passage. If we look at Deuteronomy 32:11 we will discover the method God uses. He says: "As an eagle stirs up its nest, hovers over its young, spreading out its wings, taking them up, carrying them on its wings, so the LORD alone led him…" (Deuteronomy 31:11–12).

The verse here is simple. It begins "as an eagle" and ends "so the Lord." In other words, the Lord works just like an eagle. That's His method. When we come to Him, He will take care of us. Knowing this, we ought to be excited about teaching, about tithing, and about tossing our trials and tribulations on Him.

Before an eagle bears its eaglets, it builds. And as an eagle builds, so does the Lord. How often do we see an eagle's nest? It's too high to be visible. We can see where a robin or a blue jay or a cardinal builds, but we cannot see with the naked eye where the eagle operates. She builds her nest far above the fray, far above disturbances. And she gets the best material and the best twigs to make a comfortable home for her eaglets. That's also what God does for us. He builds our lives with the best material.

Someone once said, "God doesn't make junk." That's why we cannot allow negativity to gain a foothold in our lives. When other people disparage us, we must not let their words settle in our spirit. The Bible tells us we have been "fearfully and wonderfully made" (Psalm 139:14). This is why I take little stock in people's remarks. I remember as a youngster, there were some mean neighborhood kids who used to tease me, calling me "hammerhead". However, later in life, I learned that God does not make junk. When I finally realized God doesn't make junk, I concluded I had the most handsome hammerhead in the world! It might be shaped like a hammer, but it's a strong one. It's an Ace Hardware hammer—because God doesn't make anything less.

When the Lord builds something, it's built to last. The eagle will prepare the nest with tender loving care because she understands her eaglets have to be comfortable and protected. Likewise, God builds His people. When we get a few tribulations in our lives, then, we ought to thank God, for every trial or tribulation is nothing but a brick in the building process. And we're going to need some tough bricks, because if we live long enough some storms will come our way.

So God builds His people and He also builds the church. You will remember when the disciples were on the coast of Caesarea Philippi and Jesus asked them a question: "Who do people say that I am?"

They gave various answers, but Jesus said, "Upon this rock I will build my church."

There is a method in how God does this. We are His workmen and workwomen. We do not tell God how to build His church. We do what He asks us to do. That's why, if we are on the program to preach we are to preach. If we are on the program to usher, we are to usher. If we're on the program to sing, we ought to sing. If we're a trustee or a deacon, we ought to do what we are on the program to do and stop trying to do something we're not assigned to do.

All of us are a part of the body of Christ. Each human body has two eyes, a nose, a mouth, two ears, two feet and some fingers. The hand has no business trying to hear and the ear has no business trying to talk and the mouth has no business trying to walk. We each have a responsibility and a predisposition for the particular part of the body in which we operate. And when everybody is doing his or her part, the body functions properly (1 Corinthians 12:12–26).

So God *builds*. But like the eagle, God also *breaks*. One day soon the eaglets are going to have to leave the nest—they can't stay in it forever. One thing the eagle does when she makes her nest is lay each twig horizontally so that it will be comfortable and smooth. When the eaglets have been sitting in the same place for too long, however, they are apt to get complacent. So the eagle moves a twig vertically so the nest is no longer comfortable. Now it feels more like a thicket!

Some of us may have been sitting where we're sitting for too long. So the Lord may be moving some stuff around. He knows if He doesn't, we won't move. God will send a disturbance every now and then, because some of us need to be out of the nest and flying.

An eagle *builds,* and an eagle *breaks*, but finally an eagle *bears*. As those eaglets watch their mother, beating within their breast is a desire to do what she is doing. Mother has a big job on her hand because one of those little eaglets has to be the first one out of the nest. The eaglet walks over to the edge and needs to learn the next step. Suddenly the eaglet dares to jump off, in an attempt to fly. It flutters and falls. But the good news is that the eagle mother won't let it fall too far. She swoops under it and with her wings brings it back up. Like little eaglets, we too can leave the nest. And even if we fall, we serve a God who won't let us hit the ground.

We must realize we were born to serve God. We were not born to sit, or to be depressed. We were not born to walk around with our heads hanging down. God designed us to fly, and He provides for us, protects us, and cares for us even when we fall. This is what we read in Isaiah 40:31:

...those who wait on the LORD shall renew their strength. They shall mount up with wings like eagles, they shall run and not be weary, they shall walk and not faint. — *Isaiah 40:31*

Why would an eagle need to wait? Because even the best eagle gets tired sometimes—even the best mother eagle. So there comes a time when we have to wait on the Lord. In due time we will feel our strength returning. Pretty soon we will mount up with wings like eagles. We will run and not get weary, we will walk and not faint. But first we have to wait on the Lord. If we do this, He will build us up. He may break us down, now and then, but He will never leave us. He will give us strength to go on and see what the end is going to be.

When engineers designed the Golden Gate bridge, they did so from three perspectives. They designed it first for deadweight. In other words, the bridge had to be able to endure its own weight. They also designed it to handle live weight, the traffic that goes back and forth on it. And thirdly they designed it to endure wind weight, because every now and then a storm would come and that bridge would have to endure not only deadweight and live weight but a hurricane as well.

When God made us, He made us to endure three kinds of weight: deadweight, live weight, and wind weight. First, we have to be able to endure ourselves (deadweight). Then we have to endure the stresses and strains of daily living (live weight) some of which might tempt us to put our trust in other things, or to give up on God. Then there is wind weight, representing the harshest adversities which come our way. But God has built us to endure even those!

The eagle deals with wind weight by flying above it. It uses the wind of adversity to soar to higher levels. And the higher it flies the less disturbance it experiences. At normal levels it will encounter ants and mosquitoes, humming birds, turkeys and chickens. But it can rise above all of these. Sometimes when the Lord allows adversities into our lives, it is time for us to fly higher.

Today I thank God for adversity. I thank Him that even when I am going through it, He is keeping me, protecting me, and providing for me. Hallelujah!

Use It or Lose It

If you were to ask me what was the most *famous* parable Jesus ever told I would tell you it was the parable of the prodigal son. Remember how that young man went into the far country, squandered all his money on riotous living, came to himself, went home, and found his father waiting for him?

If you were to ask me what was the most *tender* parable Jesus ever told, I would perhaps cite the story of the lost sheep, in which the shepherd went out to search for a single sheep that had gone astray. He looked in thickets, climbed jagged rocks and hunted everywhere until he finally found it. Aren't you glad we serve a God who will search for the one?

If you were to ask me what was the most *comforting* story for the helpless, I would probably choose Lazarus and the rich man. Lazarus sat outside the gate, with his clothing tattered and torn and his body wracked with disease and pain. Dogs licked his sores, and the only food he had come out of a pail of crumbs from the rich man's table. Then he died and found himself in

Abraham's bosom, where all of his misery was over and he faced an eternity free of pain and suffering.

If you were to ask me what was the most *practical* parable Jesus ever told, I would say it was the one about the talents, in Matthew 25:14. I say "practical" because this parable shows us how God treats us, how He reacts to us, and how we often respond to His blessings. It's practical because it reminds us of the way God will judge us according to the talents He has blessed us with. He said, "To whom much is given, much is required." So if God blesses us with much, He requires more of us than He does of those who are blessed with little.

A parable is an earthly story with a heavenly meaning. Jesus often told parables to make a point. And here He wanted to make a point to His disciples about His second coming. He wanted them to be ready for when He came back. He might return like "a thief in the night" (1 Thessalonians 5:2), but He *would* return.

When I was growing up in Muskegon, Michigan, we kids had the nerve to misbehave when our mothers left the house. We didn't consider that she was planning to return, but we should have acted as if we expected her to. And we ought to act right now with the understanding that Jesus is coming back.

He told this parable because He wanted His disciples to understand that He meant business about His kingdom. He also meant business about His church, and so He told the parable of the talents. We tend to think of a talent as being worth less than a dollar, but in that day a talent was worth twenty years of wages!

So the master gave these three individuals some talents. One received five talents, which was a whole lot of money. Another received two talents, and a third received just one. In other words, God blessed all of them with at least one talent. We ought to remember that if we are a born-again believer, God has blessed us with at least one talent too. This being the case, we have some responsibility before God as to what we do with it.

Now, just because you have more talents than I do, it doesn't mean you are more important than I am. A problem we have in the church is that we have five-talent Christians and two-talent Christians who think they are more important than one-talent Christians. But everybody has a role to play. Even if you have just one talent, it means something in God's program. After all it's worth twenty years of wages!

We also need to be careful about envying the talents of other people. If we have one talent and are mindful of all the two-talent and five-talent Christians, we need watch ourselves lest we start to covet what they have. With the talents God gives us comes responsibility. However we look at it, whether in terms of giftings, physical resources, financial resources, intellectual capacity, or any other resource, the more we have, the more responsible we have to be.

In the parable, the owner of the talents came back one day for an accounting, to find out what the men had done with their talents. Similarly, God will say to us, "What did you do with what I gave you?"

The first man, who had five talents, said, "Lord, I took the five talents you gave me, invested them, and got five more for you." The second one, who had two talents, said he had invested them both and doubled the master's money. But the third one admitted he had taken a shovel, gone into his backyard, and buried his one talent in the ground. In fact he'd hidden it so well that at times even *he* couldn't find it.

We know the owner had an issue with that action, or the lack of it. So he took from him what he had and gave it to the man who had had the five talents. He told the one-talent Christian, "You're lazy and slothful. You took the money that I left for you to invest and you hid it!"

If we're not careful, we could be one of those one-talent Christians in the church today. Has the Lord blessed us with a talent that we've buried in the ground? God has gifted some of us with singing ability. We may sing in the shower, in the kitchen, while we're cleaning our house and while we're working on our car, but we won't sing in God's house. Some of us have been gifted with the use of a hammer and nails. We may have built our own home and fixed things—that's real talent—but we're not willing to offer help at the church. Some of us can cook and bake, and God wants us to use this talent in His house, too.

Why does this matter? Because far too often the church needs talent, but we refuse to act like five-talent and two-talent Christians. Too often we act like one-talent Christians, failing to understand that God is expecting something from us.

Being Five-Talent Christians

I don't want to be lazy or indifferent towards the Lord, because He has been so good to me. When He comes back, I don't want Him to call me slothful. So if we're a one-talent Christian, we need to make up our mind that we will behave like the two- and the five-talent Christians.

How do we do that? Well, first we must be honest with ourselves. Which category are we in? If we realize we are a one-talent person who has hidden what we've been given, we need to find a shovel and dig fast! We need to dig up that talent so God can use it, remembering that what we have we don't own. Remember, verse 14 says the man who was setting out on his journey called his servants and *entrusted* his property to them. This means it was simply on loan.

As the Bible reminds us, we have all been bought with a price. If we're tempted to murmur, "I'm not going there" or "I'm not doing that," let's not speak too quickly. Remember, we belong to the Lord. This day, the air we breathe and everything we have belongs to the Lord. There was no doubt in the minds of those servants that the property and the money they managed still belonged to the master. Their job was to simply manage it for him. Likewise, we must remember that everything we have has been loaned to us.

*The earth is the LORD'S, and all its fullness, the world and those who dwell therein. — **Psalm 24:1***

Secondly, we must understand that God will not give us more talents than we can handle. That means, whatever the Lord has blessed us with, we *can* handle. That takes the pressure off. No matter what our gift is, God gave it to us because He knew we could handle it. We see in the current parable that the master gave one person a greater amount than he gave to another, knowing he ought to be able to handle it. Whatever He gives us, He expects us to use.

A couple of days ago, while I was meditating on this passage of Scripture, I read about a millionaire at a church meeting:

> This wealthy man rose to tell the rest of the congregation about his Christian faith.
>
> "I'm a millionaire," he said, "and I attribute it all to the rich blessings of God in my life. The turning point in my life came after I earned my first dollar, which I returned to the Lord. I believe the reason I'm a millionaire today is that I gave the Lord all I had."
>
> Everybody clapped and he sat down again. Then an older mother in the church leaned over to him and said, "I dare you to do it again."[18]

Point taken!

Then we must invest what we have been given and not sit on it. Let's look at the differences between these individuals. The first two were determined to make a profit. The third was determined not to take a loss. The first two were willing to work hard and take risks; the third was not. Sometimes in ministry we must be willing to take risks.

The first two wanted to advance the master's domain; the third had no interest in what mattered to the master. The first two viewed the money as an opportunity; the third guy saw it as a problem. The first two allowed the master's gift to change their lives; the third refused to let the gift touch his life. The first two invested, the other one wasted. The first two saw a blessing, the third a burden. The first two knew the master's will; the third hadn't a clue what God required of him.

Personally, I want to be like a two- or a five-talent Christian. I want to be somebody whom the Lord can trust with a deposit. Some of us beg the Lord to bless us, but what about the talents He has already given us? If we don't use them, we're going to lose them. If He gave us five talents, we ought to use all of them for the glory of God. If He gave us two talents, we ought to use both with the same motive. If He gave us just one talent, we can use that for the glory of God, too.

Let's not be lazy, unwise, indifferent, or stingy. Whether we are five-talent Christians or two-talent Christians, we should stop acting like one-talent Christians. At the end of the day, it's all about our faith. That's why the biblical writer says, "Where is your faith?" If we have faith there ought to be some works to prove it. Without those our faith is dead.

So the psalmist tells us to bless the Lord at all times. We are to use what the Lord has given us, and serve Him with gladness. We may not have much but we can determine to use what we have, down to our amens and hallelujahs and praise the Lords. We may not have five talents or even two talents but let's use whatever ability we have to give God some glory. Then God is pleased. That's why the Scripture says, "Give and it will be given to you: good measure, pressed down, shaken together and running over will be put into your bosom..." (Luke 6:38).

When we play sports, especially when we play football, we'll be told to "leave everything on the field." That doesn't mean we have to win the game, but it means we have to give everything we have. And the reason I'm going to give God everything is because at the end of the race, when I cross that finish line, Jesus will be on the other side with some rewards. Somebody will get a crown of life, somebody a crown of righteousness, somebody a crown of rejoicing and somebody else a crown of glory.

How many of us are running because we want to receive our crown? How many of us realize we've got to work because the Lord has been so good to us? We realize it was the Lord who woke us up this morning, and He who started us on our way. It was the Lord who put a pep in our step and clapping in our hands and jumping in our feet. He has put joy in our spirit, love in our heart, peace in our mind, happiness in our soul, and victory in life.

The final reason why we ought to give God glory, using the talent(s) He has blessed us with, is that more than two thousand years ago he went to Calvary's cross for your sins and mine. They hung Him high and stretched Him wide, and He died for our transgressions.

They took Him down from the cross and laid Him in a tomb, but early that Sunday morning He got up—with all power in His hand!

How many of us are going to serve and bless Him? I don't know about you, but I'm going to serve Him until I die. I'm going to bless His name and remain faithful, run for Jesus, and praise the Lord until my last breath.

Which servant are you?

Are We Sold Out to Christ?

A religion that gives nothing, costs nothing, and suffers nothing, is worth nothing. — **Martin Luther**[19]

The story is told of a wealthy churchgoer who had never been known for his generosity:

The church was involved in a big financial program and they resolved to pay him a visit. When the committee met with the man one afternoon, they said that in view of his considerable resources they were sure that he would like to make a substantial contribution to this program.

"I see," he said, "so you have it all figured out have you? In the course of your investigation did you discover that I have a widowed mother who has no other means of support but me?"

No, they responded, they didn't know that.

"Did you know that I have a sister who was left by a drunken husband with five children and no means to provide for them?"

No, they said, we didn't know that, either.

"Well, sir, did you know also that I have a brother who is crippled due to an automobile accident and can never work another day to support his wife and family?"

Embarrassed, they responded, "No sir, we didn't know that, either."

"Well," the man thundered triumphantly, "I've never given any of them a cent so why should I give anything to you?"[20]

Years ago, Chinese farmers decided they would eat only the big potatoes and use the small ones for seed. A new understanding of the laws of life came to them when, through their years of doing this, nature reduced all their potatoes to the size of marbles! Those farmers learned through bitter experience that they could not keep the best things of life for themselves and use the leftovers for seed. The laws of life decreed that the harvest would reflect the planting.

"Planting small potatoes" is still common practice. Too many people take all the big things of life —time, talents and treasures—for themselves and plant only the leftovers. They expect that by some crazy twist of the laws of nature, their selfishness will be rewarded with blessings.

Returning to God's Ways

People who claim to be born-again believers do not, at the core of their being, think like this. They do not go through life ignoring their stewardship responsibilities to God.

*...do you not know that your body is the temple of the Holy Spirit who is in you, whom you have from God, and you are not your own? — **1 Corinthians 6:19***

The songwriter says, "It's your thing, do what you want to do. You can't tell me who to sock it to!" But as believers we don't just do what we want to do. Our aim is to please the Lord.

*...whether you eat or drink, or whatever you do, do all to the glory of God. — **1 Corinthians 10:31***

Do you remember, when you first came to know Jesus Christ as Lord and Savior, how on fire you were? Remember how you couldn't get enough of the church? How every time they opened the doors, you were there? You gave your time, your talents, your tithes and even some love offerings. Back then you wouldn't have skipped a worship service for fear of missing a blessing, or skipped a Bible study for fear of missing a fresh understanding of God. Back then you wouldn't have dared to get up and start your day without committing it to God.

Sometimes, however, our passion can slip into a routine. It can become complacent—even dull. Before we know it, the fire, the power and the desire have waned. The answer is to return to God.

If My people who are called by My name will humble themselves, and pray and seek My face, and turn from their

*wicked ways, then I will hear from heaven, and will forgive
their sin and heal their land. — **2 Chronicles 7:14**

To rediscover the fire of our faith, we need a spiritual
awakening as never before.

*You shall love the LORD your God with all your heart, with
all your soul, with all your strength, and with all your
mind, and your neighbor as yourself. — **Luke 10:27**

Paul understood this first and greatest commandment
of Christ. If we look carefully at Romans 12:1 we see it
contains some pretty heavy stuff. Paul says that
Christians, stewards of God's resources, are to offer their
bodies. We could discuss at length what the word
'bodies' means, whether it entails minds, souls and
spirits. But it's clear that the total self is involved. And to
offer our bodies as "a living sacrifice" sounds alarming!
What does Paul mean?

The idea of a "living sacrifice" must have been quite
novel to the Jews of that day, since they had only ever
offered dead sacrifices. Remember that each year, on the
Day of Atonement, the people would bring an animal to
the priest who would kill it. That dead sacrifice was
offered as a payment for their sins.

This system didn't remain forever, though, because
Jesus Christ came as the perfect, final sacrifice. And on
the cross He died for my sins and yours. Since He was
the final substitute for our sin, there was no longer any
need for a dead sacrifice. That's why Paul said in

Romans 8:1 "There is therefore now no condemnation to those who are in Christ Jesus."

Paul continued that in view of God's mercy—in view of Jesus offering His body as a dead sacrifice—we now ought to offer our bodies as a living sacrifice. In other words, through Jesus' sacrifice on the cross, God gave us eternal life, so now we give our lives back to Him.

Fully Alive in Christ

Sometimes what we offer God is a dead sacrifice. It costs us virtually nothing when our heart is not in the offering. We may come to church only to do the time, thinking God will be happy if we just show up each week. Certainly the preacher will be happy if we show up each week, but for God, that's a dead sacrifice. The same can be true of our money. If all we do is throw money at the cause of Christ and our hearts are not alive in His work, we are offering a dead sacrifice.

By contrast, God wants a living sacrifice. He wants us to give out of a deep desire to give, out of the overflow of life that is in us. A living sacrifice is more than giving ten percent or meeting a quota of church attendance or doing time on a committee or ministry team. A living sacrifice is an offering of ourselves that flows out of an abundant life in Christ.

The famous Russian novelist, Fyodor Dostoevsky, once told how he was arrested by the czar and sentenced to die. The czar liked to play cruel psychological tricks on people who rebelled against him by blindfolding them and standing them in front of a firing squad. The blindfolded people would hear the gunshots go off, but would feel nothing. Then they would slowly realize the guns were loaded with blanks.

Dostoevsky went through this experience. He said that going through the process and believing he was really going to die had a transformative effect on him. He talked about waking up that morning with the full assurance that this would be his last day of life. He ate his last meal and savored every bite. Every breath of air he took was precious to him. Every face he saw, he studied with full intensity. Suddenly, every experience was etched in his mind. As they marched him into the courtyard, he felt the heat of the sun and appreciated its warmth like never before. Everything around him seemed to have a magical quality to it. He was seeing the world in a way he had never seen it before. He was fully alive!

When he realized he had not been shot and wasn't going to die, everything about his life changed. He became thankful for everything, even people he had previously hated. It was this experience that persuaded him to become a novelist and write about life in a way that before would never have been known to him.[21]

Christians ought to be fully alive like this. We've stared death in the face. If we are believers, then at some point in our lives we came to the understanding that our sin would lead to our eternal death. We were all doomed to die. But God sent His Son Jesus Christ to die in our place, and because of that we live. So in view of God's mercy, Paul says we are to offer our bodies as living sacrifices, to give as fully alive people of God.

Not Feeling It?

The problem with twenty-first century Christians is that we think being filled with God's power and anointing is all about how we *feel*.

"I'm not feeling that."

"I feel like they ought to do this."

"I don't feel like doing this or that."

In other words, many of us do not live as living sacrifices because we don't *feel* like it.

But Paul says in Romans 12:2, "do not be conformed to this world, but be transformed by the renewing of your *mind*, that you may prove what is that good and acceptable and perfect will of God."

He says nothing here about feelings. In fact, it is by the renewing of our minds that we are transformed. In other words, we choose whether we will conform to the pattern of this world or whether we will be living sacrifices, pleasing to God. If we are going to experience spiritual renewal in our lives, we must do more than feel it.

If we rely on our feelings to get us through, our living sacrifice will be short-lived, for feelings don't last. If we allow our giving to be directed by emotions, we will go back and forth between total commitment to Christ and conforming to the pattern of this world. Paul says we must decide, not feel, whether we will choose God's way or ours.

WORKBOOK

Chapter 3 Questions

Question: How do you respond to adversity? How should you respond?

_____

_____

_____

_____

_____

_____

_____

_____

_____

_____

_____

_____

Question: What has Jesus given you? What do you give Him?

_____

_____

_____

_____

_____

_____

_____

_____

_____

_____

_____

_____

Question: What talents are you holding back? How can you share those talents with God, the church, and those in need?

_____

_____

_____

_____

_____

_____

_____

_____

_____

_____

_____

Question: What does it mean to be a living sacrifice to God?

_____

_____

_____

_____

_____

_____

_____

_____

_____

_____

_____

_____

Question: Do your feelings hold you back from giving yourself and living completely for God? How can you overcome these feelings?

_____

_____

_____

_____

_____

_____

_____

_____

_____

_____

_____

Action: Give sacrificially, offering yourself as a living sacrifice who praises God through adversity—because He builds us up through adversity and provides for us without failing. When it comes to God's blessing, use it or lose it—don't try to hoard what He places in your stewardship. This includes talent, which the church needs, so determine to be a five-talent Christian and not hold back from God or His church body. Remember the first and greatest commandment, and be sold out completely to Christ because He gave everything to you. You are fully alive when living for Christ, so don't make stewardship or faith all about how you *feel*; make it about what you *do*.

Chapter 3 Notes

CONCLUSION

No Holding Back

When Mother Teresa visited Australia, a novice friar was assigned to be her guide and "gofer." The young man was thrilled at the prospect of being so close to this woman. He dreamed of how much he would learn from her and what they would talk about. But during her visit, he became frustrated. Although he was constantly near Mother Teresa, he never had the opportunity to say one word to her. There were always other people for her to meet.

Finally her tour was over, and she was due to fly on to Papua New Guinea. In desperation, the friar seized an opportunity to speak to the nun.

"If I pay my own fare to Papua New Guinea," he asked her, "can I sit next to you on the plane so I can talk to you and learn from you?"

Mother Teresa looked at him.

"You have enough money to pay an airfare to Papua New Guinea?" she asked.

"Oh yes," he replied eagerly.

"Then give that money to the poor," she said. "You'll learn more from that than anything I can tell you."

The problem was, the young man wanted to experience a feeling when he needed to learn by doing. By acting, he would transform his thinking, and having transformed his thinking, he would be changed to his core.[22]

That is what God wants from us—to be changed to the core. He doesn't want us to feel our way through the Christian life, fluttering back and forth between Christ and the world. He wants us to be completely sold out to Him.

Have we given everything to Him, or are we holding back? God is the supreme example of what it means to give. He gave His best for us (John 3:16), and we should do no less for Him.

God gave us the moon—and it gives;
God gave us the stars—and they give;
God gave us air—and it gives;
God gave us clouds—and they give;
God gave us the earth—and it gives;
God gave us the sea—and it gives;
God gave us the trees—and they give;
God gave us the flowers—and they give;
God gave us fowl—and they give;
God gave us the S-U-N—and the sun gives;
God gave us the S-O-N—and the Son gives;
God made men and women—
And we just ought to give![23]

REFERENCES

Notes

1. Barna, George. *The Habits of Highly Effective Churches*. Ventura: Regal Books, 1999, p. 145.
2. *Ibid*, p. 146.
3. Evans, Tony. *Tony Evans' Book of Illustrations*. Chicago: Moody, 2009.
4. Hayes Woody. In "Coach Woody Hayes." *Buckeyefansonly.com*.   2015. http://buckeyefansonly.com/woody
5. Ward, David. "If Danny Simpson Had Known More about Guns, He…." *SermonCentral*. Outreach   Inc.   September   2006. http://www.sermoncentral.com/illustrations/serm on-illustration-david-ward-stories-29127.asp
6. Carlson, Richard. *Don't Sweat the Small Stuff … and It's All Small Stuff: Simple Ways to Keep the Little Things from Taking Over Your Life*. Hachette, 1996.
7. Von Hügel, Friedrich. *Letters to a Niece*. Regent College, 2001.

8. Russell, Bob. *When God Builds a Church: 10 Principles for Growing a Dynamic Church.* Howard Books, 1994.

9. MacArthur, John. In Ron Blue, *Master Your Money* [video series workbook]. Atlanta: *Walk Thru the Bible*, 1990, p. 10.

10. Graham, Casey. "5 Reasons Why People Aren't Giving in Your Church." *Church Leaders.* ChurchLeaders.com, 2016. http://www.churchleaders.com/pastors/pastor-articles/148958-5-reasons-why-people-aren-t-giving-faithfully-in-your-church.html

11. Chappell, Paul. "God's Purpose in Giving." *Daily in the Word.* 25 October 2011, http://www.dailyintheword.org/content/god%E2%80%99s-purpose-giving

12. Evans, Tony. *Tony Evans' Book of Illustrations.* Chicago: Moody, 2009.

13. Olford, Stephen. *The Grace of Giving: A Biblical Study of Christian Stewardship.* Grand Rapids: Kregel Publications, 2000.

14. *Ibid*, p. 45.

15. Watley, William D. *Bring the Full Tithe.* Valley Forge: Judson Press, 1995, p. 58.

16. Olford, Stephen. *The Grace of Giving: A Biblical Study of Christian Stewardship.* Grand Rapids: Kregel Publications, 2000. p. 39.

17. Redpath, Alan. *The Royal Route to Heaven and Blessings Out of Buffetings: Studies in First and Second Corinthians.* CreateSpace, 2013.

18. "Best Christian Jokes." *Unijokes*. Viewed 19 January 2016. http://unijokes.com/christian-jokes/

19. Luther, Martin. In "Discipleship." *Sermon Illustrations*. http://www.sermonillustrations.com/a-z/d/discipleship.htm

20. "Preaching Daily – February 24." *Crosswalk.com*. 24 February 2016. http://www.crosswalk.com/devotionals/preaching-daily/preaching-daily-february-22-11645982.html

21. "Living the Life That Counts." *Alaska Conference of Seventh-Day Adventists*. http://www.alaskaconference.org/uploaded_assets/271573-Living_the_Life_That_Counts.pdf?thumbnail=original&1440589507

22. Coach Muller. "The Wisdom of Mother Teresa." *Good Time Stories*. https://goodtimestories.wordpress.com/2015/03/01/the-wisdom-of-mother-teresa/

23. Tan, Paul Lee. "God Made the Sun." *Encyclopedia of 7700 Illustrations*. Garland: Assurance Publishers, 1979, p. 473.

About the Author

Dr. Major A. Stewart is active in his ministry as the senior pastor of Greater Mt. Sinai Baptist Church in Charlotte, NC. Dr. Stewart is passionately involved in church leadership as a vice president of the Great Lakes Congress of Christian Education in Flint, Michigan, where he teaches the Synoptic Gospels. He is the author of *Walking in His Footsteps: A Devotional Journey in the Land of Jesus*.

Pastor Stewart is also a noted lecturer and workshop presenter on the topic of holistic stewardship. He is a certified instructor in the National Baptist Congress of Christian Education, where he teaches How To Minister to African American Males (Youth). Moreover, Dr. Stewart contributes to his community as a member of the NAACP and Alpha Phi Alpha fraternity and a board member of a public charter school.

Dr. Stewart earned a Bachelor's (BBA) Degree in Accounting and Finance from Eastern Michigan University, Ypsilanti, MI; a Master of Business Administration (MBA) Degree from California Lutheran University, Thousand Oaks, CA; a Master of Arts (MACE) Degree in Christian Education from the Michigan Theological Seminary, Plymouth, MI; and a Doctor of Ministry (D.Min.) Degree from United Theological Seminary, Dayton, Ohio. He has also completed the Church Management Certificate program at Villanova University, Villanova, PA.

Rev. Dr. Stewart and his wife, Carla, have three daughters (Alexandria Janine, Mikaela Ann, and Karissa Danielle) and live in Charlotte, North Carolina.

About Sermon To Book

SermonToBook.com began with a simple belief: that sermons should be touching lives, *not* collecting dust. That's why we turn sermons into high-quality books that are accessible to people all over the globe.

Turning your sermon series into a book exposes more people to God's Word, better equips you for counseling, accelerates future sermon prep, adds credibility to your ministry, and even helps make ends meet during tight times.

John 21:25 tells us that the world itself couldn't contain the books that would be written about the work of Jesus Christ. Our mission is to try anyway. Because, in Heaven, there will no longer be a need for sermons or books. Our time is now.

If God so leads you, we'd love to work with you on your sermon or sermon series.

Visit www.sermontobook.com to learn more.